The Circle of Sacred Dance

Peter Deunov, (Beinsa Douno) who lived in Bulgaria from 1864 to 1944, was a great and inspired teacher of the Perennial Wisdom – the thread of truth running through all the major world religions which links us to the source of all things – the Divine. All those who came into contact with him were profoundly moved by his grace and his deep spirituality. His teachings are essentially a prescription for living in harmony with others, with the earth and with the Divine, and are relevant to all people, whatever their faith or beliefs. Paneurhythmy, the form of sacred dance developed by him, is intended for all those who wish to experience harmony in their lives, for, in the sacred dance, we mirror the macrocosmic order of the heavens. As we dance the circle, we create within ourselves a still centre, and turn our spirit back to its divine source.

David Lorimer, who compiled and edited this book, is a well-known author and lecturer on spiritual matters. He is director of The Scientific and Medical Network and the International Association for Near Death Studies (U.K.). He came into contact with the teachings of Peter Deunov some five years ago and is now actively involved in his work.

To Follow Shortly

Prophet for Our Times

A Study of the Life and Teachings of Peter Deunov

David Lorimer

THE
CIRCLE
OF SACRED
DANCE

●

PETER DEUNOV'S PANEURHYTHMY

Edited by David Lorimer

E L E M E N T

Shaftesbury, Dorset • Rockport, Massachusetts

First published in Great Britain in 1991 by
Element Books Limited
Longmead, Shaftesbury, Dorset

First published in the USA in 1991 by
Element Inc
42 Broadway, Rockport, MA 01966

Note: all material used in this book has been supplied
by a group of Bulgarian followers of Peter Deunov

Cover illustration by Hanife Hassan O'Keeffe
Cover design by Max Fairbrother
Designed by Roger Lightfoot
Typeset by Burns & Smith Ltd, Derby
Printed and bound in Great Britain by
Dotesios, Trowbridge, Wiltshire

British Library Cataloguing in Publication Data
The circle of sacred dance: Peter Deunov's paneurhythmy.
1. Dancing. Related to religion
I. Lorimer, David 1952–
291.38

ISBN 1–85230–207–0

ACKNOWLEDGEMENTS

I should like to thank my Bulgarian friends for their help and
encouragement in preparing the text, my Bulgarian teacher
Katelina Green for her assistance in translating the words of
the paneurhythmy exercises, and Alma Dowle for her
beautiful drawings.

Contents

Peter Deunov

Introduction

Over the past few years there has been a renewal of interest in many traditions of sacred dance. It is part of a movement towards more 'holistic' ways of living which include care of, and respect for, the body. Many people are becoming more aware of the need for exercise and proper diet. Among the almost bewildering variety of therapies on offer, some address themselves specifically to the needs of the body in its connection to our emotional and spiritual life. The exercising of the body in dance is not only physically beneficial, but also allows us to engage in a communal and cooperative activity which can often awaken slumbering parts of our being.

The paneurhythmy sequence of exercises presented in this book is more than a sacred dance. It is based on a profound knowledge of the correspondence between sound, speech, idea and movement. All the gestures incorporated embody specific ideas and impulses heralding a new culture of Love, Fraternity and Freedom. The paneurhythmy is a poetic meditation in movement, a rite in which energy is consciously exchanged between heaven, earth and the dancers. It is not only sacred, but even sacramental, in the sense that sacraments represent the materialisation of spirit and the spiritualisation of matter.

The composer of the music and movements of the paneurhythmy is the Bulgarian Spiritual Master Teacher Beinsa Douno (Peter Deunov) who gave over 7000 lectures in the course of the thirty years from 1914 until his departure from the physical world in December 1944. These lectures cover every conceivable aspect of the Perennial Wisdom as it can be applied in our everyday lives, including many physical and mental exercises. When asked why he incarnated in Bulgaria, the Master replied that it was on account of the beautiful mountains. Summer camps in the Rila mountains became an integral part of the annual cycle of his disciples. There they met the sunrise, prayed, purified themselves, made long excursions, sang, and danced the paneurhythmy in the breathtaking beauty of the high peaks and clear lakes. It was, and is, a sublime experience which fulfils the deepest yearnings of the human soul and spirit.

According to a book by Maria-Gabriele Wosien on sacred dance, dance is the earliest art form, expressing the experience of life through the instrument of the body before using any other materials. Prior to its development into a deliberate religious rite, it was 'a rhythmic release of energy, an ecstatic act'[1]. It only gradually assumes the form of a fixed pattern of steps, gestures and poses. The second century Roman poet, Lucian, is one of the earliest exponents of a philosophy of sacred dance. He describes it as 'a thing of utter harmony, putting a fine edge on the soul, disciplining the body'[2], at once a physical exercise and a spiritual discipline.

In Hindu as well as in Western traditions, dance is associated with the Creation. Shiva, the Lord of the Dance, expresses his creative activity in dance, while Lucian writes: 'With the creation of the universe the dance too came into being, which signifies union of the elements. The round dance of the stars, the constellation of planets in relation to the fixed stars, the beautiful order and harmony in all its movements, is a mirror of the original dance at the time of creation. The dance is the richest gift of the muses to man. Because of its divine origin it has a place in the mysteries and is beloved by the gods and carried out by men in their honour'. In this sense, Davies characterises dance as 'at the same time a participation in divine activity and an imitation of that activity'[3]. Aristotle also remarks[4] that dancing is imitative; in all its forms it is 'an artistic imitation of physical movement expressive of emotions and ideas'. This definition recalls the deliberate correspondence of sound, idea and movement incorporated in the paneurhythmy.

For all the lyricism of Lucian expressed above, the prevailing climate of opinion about the state of the dance in the early years of Christianity was that it had become seriously degraded from its erstwhile sacred character; it reflected the growing moral decadence of the late Roman empire, associated as it was with sexual licentiousness and intemperance. The Church had additional reasons to be wary of the dance: not only was it intimately connected with pagan forms of worship, but it stood in marked contrast to the growing asceticism implied by the war of the soul against the flesh. As Davies observes: 'The denigration of the body now proceeded apace and where the body is vilified dance has little place except as a further demonstration of the body's degradation'[5]. If they referred to it at all, most of the early Church Fathers spoke of dance in a metaphorical fashion, paying lip-service only to the ring-dance of the angels so exquisitely illustrated in a painting by Fra Angelico of The Last Judgement[6].

Wosien links the progressive development of the mind with the diminution of spontaneity: 'Worship shifts increasingly from active physical participation – as in dancing – to a contemplative looking-on, and towards a conscious meditative internalization which excludes physical activity and even renders it unnecessary'[7]. This is certainly true of most modern Church services, although there is a good deal of evidence for dancing in Churches during the Middle Ages, in spite of earlier attitudes and strictures[8].

One of the pioneers of the modern revival of sacred dance was the legendary Isadora Duncan. It has been said of her that she returned to the ancient conception of dance as 'the mother of the arts, dance as a form of worship'[9]. She herself wrote: 'I had come to Europe to bring about a great renaissance of religion through the dance, to bring the knowledge of the beauty and holiness of the human body through its expression of movements, and not to dance to the amusement of overfed bourgeoisies after dinner'[10]. 'The dancer of the future,' she wrote, 'will be one whose body and soul have grown so harmoniously together that the natural language of the soul will become the movement of the body'[11]. Such is the impression of the paneurhythmy dancer, who will also recognise these words written at the conclusion of an article on religious dance: 'Religious dance is an expression of spiritual joy. It is a prayer, written not only with words or musical notes, but with the movement of one's whole being, body and soul, freely expanding. Indeed it can become a prayer of adoration by becoming an ecstatic meditation in the very heart of movement'[12].

The paneurhythmy exercises are certainly a prayer and an expression of spiritual joy; they are a movement and expansion of one's whole being. But they are even more: an expression of the spiritual evolution of the human soul on its journey towards perfection, and a dynamic impulse towards the unfoldment of the Aquarian Culture.

NOTES

1. *Sacred Dance*, by Maria-Gabriele Wosien (Thames and Hudson, 1974), p. 9.

2. *Liturgical Dance*, by J.G. Davies (SCM Press, 1984), p. 121.
3. *ibid*, p. 12.
4. *Encyclopaedia of Religion and Ethics* (ERE) edited by James Hastings (T&T Clark, 1918), article on 'Processions and Dances', Vol 10 p. 358.
5. Davies, *op. cit.*, p. 25.
6. Wosien, *op. cit.*, plate 20.
7. *ibid*, p. 30.
8. Davies, *op. cit.*, pp. 36 ff.
9. *ibid*, p. 77.
10. *ibid*, p. 34.
11. *ibid*, p. 148.
12. *ibid*, p. 79.

NOTE

Two days before the Master passed away, he spoke to Jarmila Metslerova–Vagarova, a choreographer, saying 'Sister, you will correct the Paneurhythmy'. Jarmila took this instruction to heart, making its fulfilment the meaning of her life. She collaborated closely with her husband Krum Vagarov to establish and describe the exact details and movements of each exercise. Krum had been in the Brotherhood since 1927, and witnessed the Master giving the Paneurhythmy exercises, as well as receiving personal instruction from him. He still dances the Paneurhythmy in his mid 80s, and has provided the basis for the description of the exercises set out in this book.

CHAPTER ONE

Who was Peter Deunov?

Bulgaria is a small, mountainous country in the Balkan Peninsula whose turbulent history has recently taken another turn with the momentous upheaval which swept across Central Europe in 1989. Twice in its history already it has given birth to a spiritual impulse which had far-reaching consequences. The first was Orphism: if one is to believe the legends, Orpheus lived in the Rhodope Mountains, south of the highest range, the Rila Mountains. This spiritual stream flowed through Pythagoras and thence to Plato and Plotinus; in the fifteenth century, the Florentine neo-Platonic revival was an essential feature of the Renaissance. The second occasion was the rise of Bogomilism in the tenth century. The word literally means 'dear to God', an epithet which Orthodox opponents found singularly inappropriate. Their approach was a mystical one, laying special emphasis on the Gospel of John. The movement migrated westwards to become Catharism in France; its brutal suppression was one of the darkest episodes of the Inquisition, but the purity and example of the Cathar initiates led indirectly to reform within Catholicism itself, largely through the offices of St. Dominic.

EARLY DAYS

Peter Konstantinov Deunov was born on the 12th of July 1864, the youngest of three children of the priest Konstantine Dunovsky. He later adopted the spiritual name, Beinsa Douno, which is used in the course of this book. His father was a well-known activist in the movement of national liberation from the Turks, which came about in 1878; he was also the first to read the Gospel in his native

Bulgarian, rather than in the original Greek, as was the rule at that time.

Few details survive about Beinsa Douno's early education. We know that he received his secondary education in Varna and went on to Suishtov, where he became acquainted with Methodism. He then taught for a while in a small village called Hatantsa before setting off for the United States in August 1888. There he studied medicine and theology in Boston and New York until his return to Bulgaria in 1895. Only a few reminiscences survive from these years. One concerns the recollections of a lawyer who had been in the U.S. at the same period and who chanced to come into a bookshop run by one of his followers around 1920. He said that the Master was very popular with the students, and on excursions used to speak to them about the beauty of Nature, the boundlessness of the universe and the grandeur of God. He would sometimes distance himself from the group, later to be found meditating or praying in a silent spot. If anyone came up and touched him, he would tremble with surprise and his face had the expression of a man awakening from a deep and beautiful dream.

In 1895, Beinsa Douno returned to Bulgaria and published his doctoral dissertation, 'Science and Education'. He then set about a systematic study of phrenology, and pursued experiments in this field throughout the early years of his itinerant teaching; he published five articles around the turn of the century. From 1897 to 1900, he was preparing himself for his work through an extended period of seclusion and meditation, spending a great deal of time in the mountains. In March 1897 he had an important revelation of his mission as a Master for all humanity, making this time of isolation and concentration all the more essential. Then in 1898 he issued a message to the Bulgarians and Slavs, saying, among other things: 'The Truth of Life descends from the world of Eternal Light to illuminate the minds, regenerate the hearts, raise and renew the souls of all the sons of Truth destined to constitute the nucleus of the new humanity of which the Slavs will be the cradle'.

THE TEACHING MISSION

In 1900, Beinsa Douno founded the Brotherhood of Light and held the first convention on the 6th of April in Varna. Outwardly, it was a small affair corresponding to the sowing of the tiny grain of wheat in the fertile soil: there were only three disciples. One of them was wondering during the lecture why the others had not arrived on time! Afterwards, the Master explained: 'Now you are only three people. But you will be many. The hall is not empty. The chairs are occupied by invisible Beings. Today is the first convention of the White Brotherhood in Bulgaria. Now you are only three men, but you will become thousands'. This last remark was indeed prophetic: the numbers of his followers were estimated at around 40 000 at the time of his death.

In the years which followed, Beinsa Douno travelled the length and breadth of Bulgaria, acquainting himself with Bulgarians and all the time teaching and healing. The annual congresses became more regular, taking place in the month of August, as they continue to do to this day. One of the places which he regularly visited was Ternovo, giving lectures on phrenology and healing. An anecdote from this period is related by a soldier in whose room he spent the night. The soldier got up in the middle of the night and went out into the courtyard, where he was astonished to see, when he looked through the window, the Master kneeling in the middle of the room. His hands were raised to heaven, and he seemed to be clothed in luminous white garments. He was praying, and the radiant light emanating from him lit up the whole room. The soldier was amazed, and inquired about the identity of this person the following morning. When informed that he was an important guest, the soldier replied: 'As I saw him last night, he didn't resemble a man, he looked like God'. The experience may have reminded the soldier of the transfiguration, when Jesus appears in his blazing body of light.

From 1905 to 1926, Beinsa Douno had his base in Sofia at 66 Opalchenska Street, where he gave his early lectures; if there was not enough room in the house, people stood outside while he lectured in the window so that all could hear. In 1914, at the outbreak of war, he was fined 25 leva for delivering lectures in war-time. He was then interned in Varna and lived in the Hotel 'Berlin', returning to Sofia in 1918. An anecdote from this time indicates the capacity which the Master had to dematerialise his physical body. For some reason or other, he had been detained in a police station, and was being sought by one of his disciples (the word *uchenik* in Bulgarian means both pupil and disciple). The disciple was accompanied by the chief of police to the cell where the Master was being held, and, when the door was opened, everyone was astonished to find the cell completely empty. The guard insisted that he had been there the whole time, and that the room had remained bolted. When the disciple finally reached the Master's house, he found him calmly sitting drinking tea . . .

From 1914 onwards, the lectures were more systematically recorded in shorthand, then later transcribed and edited for publication. The Bulgarian bibliography contains over 150 volumes, which by no means exhausts the work; it is estimated that the Master gave over 7000 lectures between 1914 and 1944. In 1922, he opened what he called his Occult School (esoteric rather than occult in normal English parlance). Lectures for the General Class were at 5 am. on Wednesdays, while the Special Class for young people took place at 5 am. on Fridays. They began exactly on time, a lesson in punctuality for the easy-going Bulgarians. The inner study phase lasted from the Autumn until the Spring Equinox, while during the Spring and Summer the lectures were followed by gymnastic exercises and paneurhythmy. Later on, in the 1920s, camps were established in the Rila Mountains during July and August, where lectures were given after sunrise at 5 am.

On Sundays at 10 am. there was a general lecture open to anyone. It usually began with a passage from the Gospel and proceeded to expound the essential spiritual message of the text. One day the Master was buying fruit in the market from a woman who had recently lost both her parents. In the course of conversation he advised her to resume reading the Bible, to which she replied that she had given up the practice years before and did not even know if there was a Bible in the house. The Master informed her that she would find one in an old chest of drawers, specifying the exact location. The woman did indeed find the Bible in the drawer, and reconstructed her spiritual life, even joining the Orthodox Church. One Sunday, she was accosted by a friend who urged her to attend a lecture by an interesting teacher. The woman protested that she really ought to go to Church, but it turned out that she could do so after the lecture. One can imagine her surprise at discovering that it was the old man who had bought the fruit who was giving the lecture! Thereafter she became a regular attender and one of his disciples.

The 1920s saw the construction of the Brotherhood Centre at Izgrev on the outskirts of Sofia. By 1926 things were sufficiently advanced for the Annual Assembly to take place there in the Summer. Some people lived in tents, while others slept out on the ground. The previous year had seen the Assembly in Ternovo, with more than a thousand people attending. The authorities were reluctant to allow the 1926 gathering to proceed, and actually proscribed the Assembly in 1927. We mention this in passing to indicate that the Brotherhood encountered considerable resistance even before the advent of Communism in 1944. From 1920 to 1928 there were Summer camps in the Moussele region. In 1929 the Assembly took place for the first time in the Seven Lakes region of the Rila Mountains. Since the war, camps have continued on a smaller scale, and in the year of writing (1990), the Assembly was held in this traditional site and was attended by over 300 people.

Throughout the 1930s and early 1940s the Master continued his schedule of lectures, whilst camps in the mountains were held until 1939, a year in which many visitors came from abroad. There were over 500 people camped by the Second Lake that year. A great deal of work was carried out by way of making paths and clearing springs, both symbolic acts. Apart from the morning lectures, there were long excursions in all weathers, and evenings round the fireside with talks and singing of the Master's songs. One evening they were singing as usual when they noticed the Master apparently fall asleep at ten o'clock. He sat up a couple of minutes later. It was only the following morning that this episode was explained when a group arrived in the camp and told of their having got lost in the dark the previous evening. Finally, at the end of their tether, they had decided to call on the Master in prayer. Shortly afterwards, they saw a light in the darkness and, within this light, the Master became distinctly visible; he indicated the right direction with a gesture of the hand. One of the brothers checked the time: it was ten o'clock, the same time that he had 'fallen asleep' at the camp.

The war was a trying time for the whole Bulgarian people. After the bombing of Sofia in January 1944, the Master moved to Marchaevo on the Mount Vitosha side of the city. His last months were full of activity. In October, Methody Konstantinov writes of a visit he made to the Master when he told him: 'I have finished my task on earth. I am going to leave'. Those close to him observed changes and a gradual withdrawal, especially at the beginning of December. A few days before his departure, Konstantinov and two others visited him. He said to them: 'What is Beethoven, what is Jesus, what is Deunov? It is only *God* who is Eternal and Boundless, only *God* is a Reality'. He then began to sing 'Aoum', making beautiful gestures – it was the last song he sang on earth.

The Master was diagnosed with double pneumonia, and breathed his last at 6 am. on the 27th of December. Among his last recorded words were 'The process must be cleared. The path for the human soul to heaven must be cleared'. In the last few hours, he said quietly and gently 'A small task has been completed', a remark of touching simplicity and beautiful humility. His body was dressed in a white suit and placed in the lecture hall at Izgrev. The musician, Maria Zlateva, writes that she was playing the violin with Acen Arnaoudov on the harp and Katia Griva singing quietly. In front of them was a table on which lay a large dish of fruit. They were playing with their hearts heavy with grief. Suddenly one apple fell out of the dish, rolled down and stopped in front of Acen's feet. Then another fell and went to Katia. Finally, a third one fell down and came to Maria herself. They all fell silent. They bent down and took the apples: 'We were grateful to the Master that he showed us his love and appreciation'.

Two days after his death, the authorities came to Izgrev with the intention of arresting the Master. But he had already left. They would certainly have detained him and probably executed him in due course. He is supposed to have said that favourable conditions for the continuation of his work would not arise for forty-five years after his death, bringing us to 1989, the year of liberation. The doctor who examined the body after death said that he had never seen such a virgin organism in all his years of practice. Because of an incident years before in which the Master had saved the life of the Communist Chief Georgi Dimitrov, the brothers and sisters obtained permission to bury his body in the garden at Izgrev. The spot is marked only with the Pentagram inscribed 'Love, Wisdom, Truth, Equity, Virtue' on the five sides. There is neither name nor dates on the tomb of this universal soul.

On the 27th of March 1945, a group of disciples met in the lecture hall of Izgrev to read a lecture, sing and pray. Eyes were directed towards the empty chair of the Master, a chair which was emphatically not empty for Pacha Theodorova, one of the stenographers. She saw the image of the Master sitting in the chair, surrounded by a blinding light. The impression lasted some time, so that it could be observed in detail: the light was composed of different lengths of rays, all of which combined to produce a vivid image of the spiritualised Master. Sometimes his face shone like the sun, while at other times intense luminous rays emanated from the whole body. The scene left an indelible impression, and is only one of many reports which indicate the Master's continuing presence and activity.

THE MISSION AND MESSAGE OF THE MASTER BEINSA DOUNO

From 1914, according to Beinsa Douno, the solar system has moved in to a purer and more spiritual region of space corresponding to what is known as the sign of Aquarius. The Culture of Aquarius will be one of harmony and reconciliation: it will see the ultimate triumph of justice and conditions for the renewal of the human soul; it will bring the Third Testament, the glorification of the Sons of God, the Testament of the disciples of the life of Universal Love. God will begin to live and manifest in a new consciousness which will make human beings aware of their real family relationships. Not that this transformation will occur overnight; it rather gives the direction of the evolution of human consciousness.

In that same year 1914 the Master spent a part of the Summer in a small village called Arbanassi, where he remained in solitude, fasting and praying. One day he was on a mountain top nearby, when Christ appeared to him and said:

Give me your body, your heart and your mind and work for me.
The Master answered:
Lord, may your will be done. I am ready.

Many people asked the Master who he was. One of his answers was as follows: 'I am a messenger from the Divine World, sent to proclaim Love and to bring its strength and power into Life. Every Divine Teacher is invulnerable. Divine Knowledge is eternal, indivisible; it was so in the past, it is so in the present, it will be so in the future. As a result, the person who has taught it, who teaches it, who will teach it, does not count. It is always the Spirit of God that counts, at all times and in all ages, and no worldly power can overcome it'.

Vessela Nestoreva comments that Great Masters represent the external relation of God to humanity. The Master is a manifestation of Divine Light. The Word flows from the Master, but belongs to God. God manifests through the Master as through no other man, because the Master lives consciously in Divine Consciousness. Hence he can truly say that the Spirit of God is speaking through him: 'I speak and do only what God tells me'. He knows that 'there exists only One Master in the world. If you want to benefit from His blessing, keep His name sacred in your mind, in your heart and in your soul. This must be the ideal of the human soul. One God exists in the world in whom you must never doubt.

Never doubt in His Love for you'. And again: 'The One who speaks down the centuries is always the same. At all times it is God who reveals Himself to humanity. The forms through which He manifests are different, but He is One'.

The following quotations amplify his mission and its source:

I have not come from my own wish, but God has sent me to work for the restoration of His Kingdom on earth. God spoke through Christ. God is speaking through me.

The ideas I am giving in the talks and lectures are taken from the Divine. What Christ said and what I am saying come from one and the same source. There are no two sources.

I have come to manifest Love and bring it to earth. This is my mission. The Truths are hidden in the lectures. I have deposited these truths there for future generations.

I am turning to you: I am the Door. The Door is Love.

The Teaching I bring to the world is not mine. It is a Divine Teaching of God. People want to extinguish this flame. That is impossible.

My purpose is to arouse the beautiful, the powerful deposited within you since time immemorial.

My task is to teach you to glorify the Living God, the source of all the goods of life, so that you may understand the meaning of life and aspire to the true culture.

The Lord of whom I speak is living in the whole of Nature, is acting in all beings; He speaks inwardly to each soul, to each heart. I am in constant contact with Him. I know His voice, I preach His Teaching, I accomplish His Will, I obey His Spirit, and my joy lies in His Living Word.

In a lecture on The Master, Beinsa Douno states that the true Master is free in the complete sense of the word; he comes to the earth as a messenger of heaven to fulfil a Divine mission; absolute truth permeates the whole of his being. Among the nation in which he incarnates, only few recognise him for what he is: a first group, indifferent and spiritually retarded and whose Divine feeling is dormant, see nothing unusual in him. A second group who are slaves of their passions feel reproached by the purity of his life and begin to disdain and persecute him. A third group notice something mysterious in him but are sluggish and prefer sleep to spiritual work. A fourth group see his light but not in its true essence, accepting him as an adept or magician according to their studies. Finally, only a small group see and feel something unusual about him; they try to study him and enter into his path by applying virtues and developing the qualities of the disciple: love, light, peace, joy.

The Master remains 'most unknown to people, most humble and most puzzling. Only he can say with conviction: "I am nothing in myself" ', even though he is master of his mind, heart and body, as well as of the elements. He works in silence, sowing the seeds of the new culture. One day he came up to a group of disciples and told them: 'I can raise the dead; this is within my power. I can heal all illnesses; this is also within my power. But what is the use?'. He then went on to tell a parable about a little pig. Suppose he pulled this pig out of the mud and scrubbed it clean so that its skin was nice and pink. Where would this pig go as soon as he was released? Why, straight back into the dirtiest swamp! Is this a worthwhile way to work?

Suppose now, he continued, that I set myself up in a capital city like London, Rome, Berlin, Moscow or Istanbul and began treating the sick. My fame would soon spread to the four corners of the earth, and there would be tremendous traffic jams of people bringing the infirm for treatment; doctors who would come to research and study, journalists to write sensational articles, tradesmen and makers of souvenirs, followed by all kinds of entertainers. Besides, those cured might continue their former way of life and bring on another illness. What would be the use? What is requred is a point of leverage and a lever. Like Archimedes, I say: 'Give me a point of leverage in which to place my lever and I will modify the orbit of life'. The point of leverage is the disciples, and the lever the Teaching, which can be presented to all beings of good will. They will realise that it brings joy, health, well-being, knowledge, love and the meaning of life.

It is interesting to note the opinion of René Guenon about the Master Beinsa Douno. Guenon was the foremost exponent, along with Ananda Coomaraswamy, of the Perennial Philosophy in the thirties and forties, a tradition continued by Frithjof Schuon and S.H. Nasr. Guenon wrote: 'He is the real messenger of Heaven. He is the greatest person who has come down to the earth. He did not come to create a new religion, of which there are already enough; neither did he come with a new science or with the intention of founding a social movement. He is the greatest spiritual magnet yet able to appear on the earth. He will magnetize his disciples with the magnetism of love, and they in turn will transmit this magnetism to humankind as a whole'. There was also an exchange between Sophrony Nikov, the president of the

Theosophical Society in Bulgaria, and Krishnamurti at a convention in Holland. Readers will probably know that Krishnamurti was proclaimed to be the Messiah by the Theosophical Society, a title which he later repudiated. After the talk, Nikov went up to Krishnamurti and took the liberty of asking him whether there was any incarnated Master in the world. His reply was that there was one in Bulgaria.

ESSENTIAL TEACHINGS OF BEINSA DOUNO

As mentioned above, the Master came to preach the Teaching of Christ, the application of which will be the basis of the new culture. One of his commandments was:

> Love the perfect way of Truth and Life.
> Place Goodness as the foundation of your
> home,
> Righteousness as the standard proportion,
> Love as the adornment,
> Wisdom as the rampart,
> Truth as the Light.
> Only then will you know Me
> And I shall manifest Myself to you.

The aspiration of the disciple is contained in the following prayer:

> The disciple should have:
> A heart as pure as a crystal
> A mind as radiant as the sun
> A soul as vast as the universe
> And a spirit as mighty as God and one with
> God

'Three things concern me', he said. 'The Love of God concerns me, the Wisdom of God concerns me and the Truth of God concerns me. I am concerned with the Will of Love about which I have spoken to you. Salvation is in our hands'.

'We preach the Christ of Love, which sustains and fills every heart; we preach the Christ of Wisdom, which enlightens every mind; we preach the Christ of Truth, which liberates and elevates the world!

God is Love, Wisdom and Truth. Christ is the manifestation of God. He is the Son of God.

Christ is Divine Love, Divine Wisdom and Divine Truth, which all men and women need to apply. The whole of humanity must know, study and apply these principles:

> The first principle on which the whole of existence is based is Love; it brings the impulse to life; it is the compass, the stimulus within the human soul.
>
> The second principle is Wisdom, which brings knowledge and light to the mind, thus enabling human beings to use the forces of Nature in a noetic way.
>
> The third principle is Truth; it frees the human soul from bondage and encourages her to learn, work well and make efforts towards self-sacrifice.
>
> There is nothing greater than these principles; there is no straighter or surer path. In these three principles lies the salvation of the world!
>
> Love in the heart brings purity, thanks to which the capacities latent within human beings will develop, enabling them to achieve all their noble desires.
>
> Wisdom in the mind brings light which helps us in the study of the laws of Nature.
>
> Truth shining within the soul brings freedom from every weakness and vice.
>
> Love eliminates hatred, violence, murder.
>
> Wisdom eliminates ignorance, error, darkness.
>
> Truth eliminates lies, slavery, sin'.

'Absolute purity, sincerity, justice and kindness is demanded of you all; abandon all duplicity and egotism. You are invited to become examples of the new man and the new woman. You must have a disinterested love, an unshakeable faith and an incorruptible will! This teaching which I am giving you has been tried and tested; it contains the fundamental rules according to which one must live.

The Old Testament is for children; the New Testament is for adults; and the Third Testament, which is now on its way, is for the Sons of God, who will bring into the world Love, Wisdom and Truth.'

'To pray is to direct one's mind, heart, soul and spirit towards the Source of Life from which we have emerged . . . Why do you pray to God? God is Love. Can you add something to Him by your prayer? We pray to God because He is perfect. Therefore we can only direct a good, radiant thought towards the One Who loves us and thank Him. We send our gratitude to the Perfect and Loving One. We cannot give Him anything more.

Think of God, that you may become perfect like Him.
Think of God, that you may become good like Him.
Think of God, that you may become kind like Him.

The only thing you can do is to manifest your love of God to your neighbour and all your brothers and sisters, mothers and fathers, even down to the tiniest plants and insects'.

'From one end of the world to the other, a single song must be heard – the song of the fulfilment of the love of God.

The New is coming into the world. The New is in the
song.
The New which is coming into the world is in the thought.
The New which is coming into the world is in the heart.
The New which is coming into the world is in the soul.
The New which is coming into the world is in the Spirit.
Everyone must obey their mind.
Everyone must obey their heart.
Everyone must obey their soul.
Everyone must obey their Spirit.
This is the language of God.
This is the call sent forth to all the people in the world
today'.

Some passages on the great purpose of life are as inspiring as they are powerful and profound:

Youth is a garment of life.
Light is a garment of knowledge.
Water is a garment of health.
Life without virtues is like
A garden without flowers
Or trees without fruit.
The beginning of all things is the Spirit.
The beginning of the Spirit is Love.
The zenith of the Spirit is Wisdom.
The end of all things is Truth which brings freedom.
There is only an end where all contradictions cease.
There is only a beginning where all is in accord.
If the heart does not feel, the beautiful cannot come.
If the mind does not think, the Great will remain unknown.

When the wise man enters the boat, it starts of itself.
Why must you suffer? In order that joy may come.
Why must you live? In order to acquire happiness.
Why must you be beautiful? In order that Love may visit you.
A beautiful thought, a noble feeling, a good act are loyal
friends.
The real friend must be beautiful, noble and good.
Give ear to the instructions of your Spirit
And the directions of your soul, that you may be well at all
times.
The faith and hope of man are tested in the path of life.
The mind and will of man are tested in the path of
knowledge.
The nobility of the soul and the mercy of the heart
Are tested in the path of freedom.
One is the Spirit, many are the spirits.
One is God, many are the souls.
One is He, many are His sons and daughters.
One is the Name of the Whole,
Numberless are the names of the parts.
Walk where the light walks.
Descend where the water descends.
Work where the Spirit works.
Love lives.
Wisdom shines.
Truth brings what is to be'.

* * *

'The man of Love is in the Truth; not he that speaks about love, but
rather he who carries it within his soul.
The man of Wisdom is in the Light; not he who speaks about
wisdom, but rather he who carries it within his Spirit.
The man of Virtue is within the creative, Cosmic Will; not he who
speaks about virtue, but he who carries it within his heart.
Where is the Truth?
Where the soul, the spirit and the heart are free.
Apply:

    The Living fire of Love
    The Living light of Wisdom
    The Living power of Truth
    Love out of which life springs forth is true Love
    Wisdom out of which light emanates is true Wisdom

Truth whence freedom comes is Truth indeed.
The Spirit reigns therein.
God is light in which the fruits of Virtue ripen.
Great ideas dwell in noble souls.
Radiant and brilliant thoughts in radiant and brilliant
minds.
Pure desires in pure hearts.
We shall speak forth to the diligent disciples
With the beaming rays of light
In the presence of Love, Wisdom and Truth.
May Love, Wisdom and Truth abide with you
Now and throughout eternity.
May they sustain and illumine
All that is good and sublime within you.
These are the words of life.
Blessed are those who walk in Wisdom,
For they shall abide in the Light.
Blessed are those who live in the Truth,
For they shall be freed from the chains of all limitations.
This is the Eternal Testament of the Spirit.'

Finally, the blessing of the Master Beinsa Douno:

> May Love abide within you.
> The Love which brings peace, joy and
> gratitude.
> May the Love of the Holy Spirit shine within
> you.
> Rejoice in the Spirit.
> The sun of life is radiance eternal.
> May my peace abide in you
> Who dwell in divine purity.
> May my Light and Love be always within you,
> Disciples of life!

CHAPTER TWO

The Background to Paneurhythmy

In this chapter we shall discuss three aspects of the Teaching of Beinsa Douno which have a direct bearing on the principles and practice of the paneurhythmy: his philosophy of Nature, because the exercises are, as we shall see, an exchange of energy between human beings and Nature; his ideas on music, since the paneurhythmy music which he composed needs to be understood in the context of the other songs and melodies which he composed; and his teaching on the meaning of gesture and movement, as the paneurhythmy exercises are a systematic series of bodily gestures.

NATURE

If the fundamental principles of the message of Beinsa Douno are Love, Wisdom and Truth, one of its most prominent practical aspects is the development of a conscious relationship with Nature through attending sunrise, spending time in the mountains, through nutrition and exercise, and, of course, through the practice of paneurhythmy itself. Unlike traditional Christianity in the West, the health of the physical body is not ignored in this Teaching, but is regarded as an important precondition of spiritual health.

We are currently living through an intellectual transformation in our ideas about Nature, many of which date back to the seventeenth century scientific revolution. Prior to that time, and more especially in traditional societies where animism prevailed, the earth was considered as alive. The Neo-Platonic hermetic philosophers saw the earth as a living organism in which humanity was embedded. Seventeenth century philosophy popularised a mechanical outlook on the basis of a universe which operated as a giant clockwork system. From this angle, Nature was an inanimate mechanism to be exploited for human gain, and the human body itself came to be seen as a machine with various moving parts like hands as levers and the heart as a pump. The brain was likened to a computer, and it is even seriously argued today that it could in principle be entirely replaced by computer chips.

Although most molecular biologists like to think of themselves as mechanists, there is an alternative school emerging which considers that human development cannot be satisfactorily explained by genetic programmes alone. They advance the idea of human beings as self-regulating organisms, a concept which has been extended to the planet by James Lovelock's 'Gaia Hypothesis'. There is much talk about the Rebirth of Nature, which really means the rebirth of an organic understanding of Nature. From this angle, the mechanistic view looks like a temporary aberration which is now being supplanted by the more traditional model.

The ecology movement is gradually penetrating not only the upper reaches of economics and politics, but also the ecclesiastical establishment who are busy formulating Green Christianity and a corresponding Green Spirituality. The human relationship with Nature is now at the top of the agenda after centuries of neglect. All this is by way of preface to describing Beinsa Douno's Teachings which were being disseminated decades before the above developments had occurred.

He begins by observing that we have generally become alienated from Nature, and cannot participate in its work without completely altering our attitude and understanding. Nature, he writes[1], 'is not only a world of physico-chemical processes regulated by mechanical laws, nor is it an inanimate mechanism acted upon by blind forces. It is not only a source of energies which mankind tries to use for purely material ends which are very often entirely contrary to Nature's real goals. Nor is it simply a treasury of boundless wealth which we are allowed to dispose or waste according to our whims'.

He goes on to define Nature in the real sense of the word: 'Nature is an aggregate of noetic* beings of different degrees of development and diverse levels which are acting in perfect unity and complete harmony. The work of these beings is wisely distributed in the various realms of the cosmos, and when one

* noetic here signifies the higher reason or intellect

speaks of the work of Nature, one is actually referring to the work of these highly intelligent beings which are to be found behind everything which happens not only on earth but in the whole world, whether or not it is visible to us'. Contemporary people only see the results of this activity in the mineral, vegetable, animal and human kingdoms and jump to the premature conclusion that it can all be explained as an automatic mechanism.

The consequence of this 'false understanding' is that it prevents us from establishing a conscious link with these intelligent beings. How can we set up any communication with beings whose existence we categorically deny? Through observation of, and participation in, the work of Nature, we can re-establish this link and gain precious insights into the nature of life itself. When asked about the books in his library, Beinsa Douno replied that Nature was his library and the source of his knowledge about the school of life. To the modern scientific understanding of the earth as alive, we add here that natural processes are regulated by intelligent beings with whom we can enter into contact. The reader can experiment in this regard by sitting quietly beside a plant or tree and allowing conscious communication and dialogue to emerge. The results can sometimes be quite unexpected!

Greeting the Sunrise

One of the customs of the White Brotherhood between the Spring and Autumn Equinoxes is to meet the sunrise. Beinsa Douno began this practice in the 1920s as part of a programme to bring his followers into closer contact with Nature. In the Rila Mountains, the spectacle is both mystically beautiful and movingly majestic. Such moments are etched in the memory of anyone who has seen the sun come up over the Balkans with the wispy grey contours of other mountain ranges in between. The ideas underlying this practice are explained in an essay on the influence of solar energy[2].

The exchange of energy between the sun and the earth takes place through a process of polarisation. Energy is received through the negative pole and transmitted through the positive; when a centre of energy is positive, it gives out, and when negative it receives. Positive energy is creative or masculine, and negative energy constructive or feminine. These principles of giving and receiving underpin the whole philosophy of paneurhythmy. In relation to the earth at any given point of its axis, it receives more between midnight and midday, and gives out more between midday and midnight. The maximum flow of positive energy from the earth occurs at sunset.

By the same token, the earth is at its most receptive during the early morning dawn period. Beinsa Douno recommends that we take into consideration the following law: 'That we are an integral part of the earthly organism, which means that we receive when the earth does, and inversely, we give out when the earth does so'. It is at this time that the human organism is at its most receptive, hence the powerful effect of the first rays from the sun. The energy in question here is the vital or subtle energy which Eastern philosophers call *prana* and which is at its most abundant at dawn.

A further analogy emerges when we consider the cycle of the seasons. This *prana* and these solar rays do not operate at the same intensity throughout the year. At the beginning of Spring, the earth is at its most receptive in the respective hemisphere, and the concentration of *prana* is at its greatest – organisms can therefore absorb a greater quantity, as is reflected in the surge of growth which takes place in the three months following the 22nd of March. The earth moves into its most creative phase. During this period we too can absorb the *prana* and work consciously not only on our bodily health, but also on our inner growth through activation of our thinking and feeling in this energy exchange process: 'We must sense in all the fibres of our being a grateful tenderness for this life-giving force which completely envelops us; we must open up with love in order to receive its beneficial influence which brings a renewal of strength and a new freshness to our thoughts and feelings'. The budding and blossoming of the plants corresponds to a pure joy arising in the soul.

Excursions and camps in the Rila Mountains began in the early 1920s, and in 1929 the first camp was organised in the Seven Lakes region. The rationale was for Beinsa Douno and his followers to spend a period of time in closer contact with Nature and to free themselves from everyday cares and limitations. The Rila Mountains are the highest range in the Balkans and are not far from the Rhodopes, where Orpheus is said to have roamed. The clarity of the light and the purity of the air combine to produce scenes of stunning beauty. One of the finest views is to be found on a grassy plateau overlooking the two Maritsa lakes, just below the source of the river itself. To dance paneurhythmy on this spot is an inspiration indeed!

While the modern camps are equipped with waterproof tents and warm sleeping bags, the same cannot be said of the early

Fig 1.   *Paneurhythmy being performed in the Rila Mountains*

excursions where people slept out around fires come rain or shine
The weather in the Rila Mountains can switch from summer to
winter in a matter of hours. When the sun shines it is hot and
bright, but later on a day which began wonderfully, the fog and
mist can come down, followed not long after by torrential rain. Part
of the teaching imparted by the mountains is the capacity to
appreciate all kinds of weather, just as one comes to accept the
difficulties as well as the joys of life. At the Moussala camp we still
climb about 1000 feet at 5 am. in order to meet the sunrise. In the
old days, though, the ascent was nearer 2000 feet up to the summit
of Moussala. The climb began at about 3.30 am. Climbing the
mountain for sunrise is a spiritual as well as a physical exercise
typical of the integrated approach to be found in Beinsa Douno's
Teaching.

He explains that 'the mountains are accumulators of energy and
man represents a transformer. When you go to the mountains you
must know how to transform the energy it gives you, otherwise
you will gain nothing'. The peaks of the mountains are points
where cosmic energy is transformed and distributed for work on
earth. It is in the mountains that one can acquire the inner spiritual

aspect of this energy through meditation and prayer as well as through paneurhythmy. If one reaches an awakened and elevated state of consciousness there occurs an intense circulation and exchange of physical and spiritual energy through contact with the living forces of the Beings of Light who are to be found in the peaks.

The key to benefiting from a trip to the mountains is purity. Up there the air and water are pure, as is, relatively speaking, the atmosphere. It is recommended to perform breathing exercises and to drink plenty of hot water. This water maintains a stable internal temperature as well as purifying the system. It is taken straight from one of many springs which have been cleaned and set up by the Brotherhood over the years. There is a special spring near the Second Lake which bears an inscription and gives its water through a spout of cupped marble hands, symbolic of the water of life described in the Gospel of John.

A final link with Nature is through nutrition, a kind of alchemy whereby energy is transformed from one state to another. Beinsa Douno recommended pure, fresh vegetarian food, and especially fruit in which a great deal of solar energy has been accumulated. Food should be eaten slowly and with a sense of contentment and gratitude so as to absorb not simply the physical energy but also the *prana*. The following formula sums up his advice:

> Break the bread with Love, and reflect that God is within it
> Drink the water with Love, and reflect that God is within it
> Breathe the air with Love, and reflect that God is within it
> Contemplate the light with Love, and reflect that God is
> within it.

Meals in the mountains, as elsewhere are always preceded and followed by the short formula 'The Love of God brings fullness of life'.

MUSIC

Music played an essential part in the life of Beinsa Douno, as well as in his Teaching. He began to study the violin in his youth, and was told by his relatives that 'the violin does not provide a man with food', and that the study of music was not an indispensable feature of life. His own experience advised him differently, as he pursued his studies first with a good technician, and then with a

Czech whom he describes as a musician of genius. By the time he visited America as a student, he was already giving small concerts to his fellows.

He used occasionally to bring his violin into the lecture hall. Even the act of taking the instrument out of its case and cleaning it was performed with great finesse. It is said that he played softly, without any great technical flourishes, and that his light touch produced a sound which was pure, clear, delicate and exquisite. The sounds awakened noble and profound images in the audience. Sometimes he improvised melodies and variations, giving the impression of a flowing mountain spring. Songs were even created in the course of the class, and then written down by one of the many musicians present.

There is a touching story of an occasion in the mountains when someone asked Beinsa Douno to sing a song that he had never sung. After a period of silence, the Master took up his violin and sang 'The Song of the Stranger' which the witness describes as a prayer of unusual beauty tinged with sadness. Many of his melodies convey an impression of the soul's nostalgia for her homeland of light. Although the melody has been lost, the words were transcribed:

> I am a stranger in this world.
> I know no one besides Thee.
> Thou, my Lord and my God hast created all things for
> me.
> I offer my gratitude unto thee.
> Upon Thee, Lord, have I placed my confidence.
> May my prayer rise to Thee'.

In the song book published in Bulgaria, there are about about 200 songs and melodies composed by Beinsa Douno, in addition to all of the music for the paneurhythmy. In the Rila Mountain camps, songs are sung with prayers at dawn, and again in the evening at nightfall. It is an exquisite moment when one hears the notes wafting up towards the rocks, with some of the words in an ancient, almost untranslatable language which cannot be sullied by profane associations. At the Izgrev centre in Sofia, some songs were sung at the time of lectures and meals. They permeate the consciousness in a way which tends to purify the mind of the incessant chatter which arises only too spontaneously in our vacant moments.

The main focus of Beinsa Douno's teaching about music was concerned with its transformative effects and consequently with its role in the establishing of the new culture of Love. Some of his writings give fresh insights into the nature and function of music, such as his assertion that music is the highest form of intelligent expression because it is condensed light; and light is an expression of thought. This leads him to comment on the relationship between possessing an inner musical sense and thinking correctly, since the resulting thought will be a harmonious chord. Another example elucidates the role of music in purifying the feelings, just as breathing is necessary for the purification of the blood.

Three kinds of music are distinguished: the mechanical, which is correlated with technique and applies only to the animation of inert things; organic music, which organises living matter; and psychic (or soul) music which awakens the hidden capacities of the human soul. What is called 'occult' music (a better term in English would be 'spiritual') combines these three qualities and will be a driving force in the renewal of culture. The new spiritual music is characterised by the gradual development of its process from the fundamentals upwards, by the harmony obtaining between notes and words, and by its extreme tenderness, naturalness and clarity which gives rise to living images in the hearer. The overall effect is an organisation and coordination between thoughts, feelings and actions.

In its broadest sense, music means harmony in one's thoughts, feelings and desires: 'When a person possesses this music within themselves, they feel something singing softly inside, in the depths of the soul. They taste a continous harmony which calms the soul and mind, and which impresses a new direction on the thoughts'. Beinsa Douno encouraged his followers to sing and play musical instruments not only as a contribution to physical health, but also as a means of transforming negative energies into positive ones and of balancing thoughts and feelings. Its effects he summed up as follows: 'Music brings expansion to the soul; strength and power to the Spirit; gentleness and warmth to the heart; freedom and light to the mind'.

At another level, the supreme goal of music is 'to kindle the sacred fire of Love in the human soul'. The task of the musician is to console and raise afflicted and fallen souls and prepare them for the advent of a new order of Love: 'Love is music – harmony – in the whole of life. In all circumstances, however unfavourable, those aspiring towards the new life should make an effort to sing, play and listen to good music; the result will be the establishment of an inner harmony which will enable the person to call upon the luminous assistance of higher beings, essential for inner peace and a balance and attunement between one's heart and thoughts'.

Beinsa Douno explains that everything in Nature vibrates and produces a tone. In that sense, nature is a gigantic orchestra, as indeed are the individual organs of the physical body. There is the music of the wind in the trees, of the sea, of flowing water, of birds and animals; there is even a special music of the opening of the petals of a flower, or the ripening of fruit in the orchard. The most beautiful concerts, for those capable of perceiving them, are those accompanying the sunrise, as Blake maintained two hundred years ago. The Master tells us that the Angels are in the process of opening the musical centres of human beings so that they become aware of angelic music and the music of the spheres. This last kind is open to those who have attained cosmic consciousness, a veritable symphony which resounds through space and which reveals the meaning of life to those who have ears to hear it. The whole universe – the sun, the earth, the stars – has its song.

The music of the new culture will have more powerful and beneficial effects than present-day music. Beinsa Douno explains that it will descend from a higher world and will first be received through the antennae of the finest human beings. It will give a potent impulse towards the manifestation of goodness in all areas of life; it will bring more light, more inspiration of mind, heart and will through the level of spiritual contact implied in the link between composer and advanced beings. The performer and composer are both stimulated and inspired by beings in the invisible world – when he was composing, Beethoven was in the presence of elevated musical beings who were directing his thought and creative sense. The listener to the songs of Beinsa Douno will gain an impression in the depths of their being that his music is a materialised form from the Divine world of harmony, beauty, light and purity.

The music which accompanies the paneurhythmy was written with the foregoing principles in mind. As explained in the next chapter, it is based on a close correspondence with the movements and the idea being expressed. Its qualities surpass those of ordinary music in that it is an embodiment of the ideas of the new culture and it directly addresses and awakens the highest human faculties. It leads the person to the highest spheres, to which they have always aspired in their most sacred moments; they are united

to the real world'. Such music is a transmitter of vitality and health
and a spur to the practical realisation of what Beinsa Douno calls
'The High Ideal' of the path to perfection.

GESTURE AND MOVEMENT

Followers of the Master Beinsa Douno describe his whole
disposition and gait as musical, in accordance with his own
recommendation that 'the body must vibrate and move musically;
every gesture must be musical'. Each gesture, he explains, is the
expression of a particular thought, feeling or energy. The gestures
of a calm person are quite different from those of someone who is
agitated, anxious or fearful; many are unconscious and perhaps
even unnecessary.

The ultimate aim is to accomplish each movement and action
consciously. A movement is perfect when it expresses the
satisfying combination of the forces of the spirit, the heart, and the
thoughts. Disharmonious movements are the reflection of an as yet
uncoordinated consciousness. The work of the disciple is the
education and mastery of limbs and movements. We are constantly
reacting to internal and external stimuli and consequently making
unconscious and superfluous movements.

If every idea and quality of soul corresponds to a certain
movement or gesture, it is clear that there are movements which
express kindness, mercy, justice, Love, beauty and other virtues.
Each virtue has its own line of movement. The gestures
incorporated in the paneurhythmy exercises are dynamic
expressions of the ideas which they embody. Some, like 'Giving'
and 'Ascending' are obvious, while others reveal their deep
meaning in the course of practice. The same principles are applied
in the other gymnastic exercises given by the Master, where the
movement corresponds with the formula: a variant of 'Providence'
invokes a blessing on the exerciser through the gesture of bringing
one's hands down over the head and down to the sides. In the next
chapter we shall refer to the signifance of starting the exercises on
the right foot, representing the masculine, creative principle. This
can be extended to beginning every enterprise, whether getting out
of bed or leaving the house, on the right foot, so that the creative
principle is expressed before the constructive principle. In the
process of giving and receiving expressed in the paneurythmy, the
gestures of arms and legs represent a flowing exhcnage between

these principles as they are represented in the dancers and in Nature.

NOTES

1. Translated from 'Comment on Entre dans l'École de la Nature' from *La Vie pour le Tout*, pp. 119 ff. (Paris, Le Courrier du Livre, 1955/1989)
2. See lecture 'L'Influence de l'Energie Solaire' in *Dans le Royaume de la Nature Vivante*, pp. 7ff. (Paris, Le Courrier du Livre, 1954/89)

Other sources used include an essay on Music from 'L'Enseignement de Vie Nouvelle' pp. 213 ff. (Paris, Le Courrier du Livre, 1983), various essays in the periodical *Le Grain de Ble* and other unpublished manuscript material.

CHAPTER THREE

The Essentials of Paneurhythmy

MEANING

In the widest sense, paneurhythmy means the great universal harmony of movement in the whole cosmos. The scope of this statement can be appreciated by considering the following kinds and scales of movement:

- the movements of the planets
- the undulating movement of light waves
- the currents of the electromagnetic field
- the spinning of atoms and electrons
- the transformative motion in the tips of roots and shoots in plants
- the pumping of the heart and the circulation of the blood

These kinds of movements are both creative and integrative – they regenerate and construct everything in nature, producing countless forms through such ceaseless activity.

In a narrower sense, paneurhythmy is a noetic exchange, a giving and receiving, between the living forces of human beings and nature through the three series of exercises described in the next chapter. The link between these two definitions of paneurhythmy is the fact that if human movements are in harmony with the rhythm of cosmic movements, then the dancer is linked with the forces of living nature which are then absorbed.

Etymologically, the word paneurhythmy (not to be confused with the eurythmy of Rudolf Steiner) is a combination of three roots:

1. *Pan* – meaning the whole or cosmic, symbolises the creative masculine principle, the seed.

2. *Eu* – meaning true or supreme, the essence from which everything arises, symbolising the feminine, receptive and constructive principle of nourishment, the form.
3. *Rhythmy* – meaning periodicity or correct regularity of movement, the organising principle.

The threefold division of the word corresponds to other aspects of Beinsa Douno's Teaching:

Mind	Heart	Will
Thinking	Feeling	Acting
Wisdom	Love	Truth/Freedom
Creative	Constructive	Organising
Brain	Thorax	Limbs/Muscles
Form	Content	Meaning

Some of these links are explained in the following quotation:

> When we think correctly, that is to say, when our thinking is straight and just, we possess all the appropriate forms in which we can place the Divine Content of Life. As soon as we possess this content, our heart (the feelings) will freely express its qualities and will stimulate the inner strength which gives Meaning to life. This Meaning enables the human will to function properly: only when we use our will judiciously will our life have a meaning.
>
> Correct thinking, feeling and acting is an indispensable condition for the balanced working of the mind, the heart and the will. One needs to know that the Form is necessary for the expression of the Content; and the Content is indispensable to the expression of the profound inner meaning of life itself. Form, content and meaning are therefore closely linked: the form with the mind, the content with the heart, and meaning with the human will.

These correspondences will be further elaborated when we consider the principles below. At this stage it is sufficient to note that dancing the paneurhythmy implies a close connection and correlation between mind, heart and will. Another definition of paneurhythmy refers to it as the science of harmonious movements linked to human thoughts and feelings; indeed, it follows that the most perfect performance of the paneurhythmy achieves precisely this coordination of thought, feeling and action.

For reasons explained in the previous chapter on Nature, the dancing of paneurhythmy takes place between the Spring and Autumn Equinoxes. It is danced in a circle, symbol of the great wheel of life. Of this circle, Beinsa Douno said: 'Souls are unified by the living circle, obstacles keeping people apart are done away with, and strong links are re-established. The circle is the expression of Beauty and Unity'. The correct performance of the exercises enable us to be permeated by the positive forces of nature, and the love of God will link the dancers in the infinite circle and cycle of nature.

PRINCIPLES

There are seven principles which underlie the paneurythmy exercises.

1. The Principle of Intelligence

This states that every phenomenon is underpinned by intelligence and the higher noetic reason. We saw in the last chapter how Beinsa Douno's philosophy of nature depicted the processes as both living and intelligent.

2 The Principle of Correspondence

This principle can be elucidated by saying that there are analogies and correspondences between all created phenomena. Hermetic philosophy expresses this truth with the dictum 'As above, so below', transposed by Beinsa Douno into the terms 'As within, so without'. Obvious correspondences arise with the natural processes of birth and death, the passing of the seasons compared with the ages of life, and the ebb and flow of tides when compared with the inner movement of our thoughts and feelings. In music we find correspondences between the notes of the different octaves, while in chemistry there are correspondences within the periodic table of the elements. It is important to realise, though, that the existence of such correspondences implies an underlying unity and connectedness of the corresponding parts: sound in the case of music, and a common atomic substructure in the case of chemistry.

When specifically applied to paneurhythmy, the important correspondences are between the tone of the music, the form of the movement and the content of the idea expressed in the words actually sung in a few exercises. The coordination of music, ideas and movement is far from arbitrary. Beinsa Douno deliberately coordinated these three on the basis of the principle of correspondence, making the combination much more potent than any single element. The movements and music carry the idea within them, making the exercises embodied ideas. Such correspondences are explained in more detail in the descriptions given of individual exercises.

Beinsa Douno explains that, in the ancient mystical schools, songs are accompanied by movements. Such schools knew of the powerful impulses generated by words, music and movements carried out simultaneously. Certain formulae were accompanied by songs and special movements which exerted a potent influence on the performer. Some of the gymnastic exercises invented by Beinsa Douno and executed before the paneurhythmy are similarly combinations of gestures with appropriate sacred formulae.

A further correspondence exists between the exercises and our consciousness, so that a definite effect on the mind and heart is produced by a specific exercise. In general, they are linked with the process of the awakening and liberation of the creative faculty of the human soul in its quest for perfection. The correspondence of inner and outer mirrors that between the physical, spiritual and divine worlds or body, soul and spirit. The paneurhythmy dancer is operating in all three worlds at once; it is the paneurhythmy itself which links and unifies them.

3 The Principle of Vibration or Movement

Movement is life. Without movement, life cannot manifest. Everything is moving and vibrating at a specific frequency. Our senses are designed to perceive a small spectrum of the total frequency band of sound and light. Only clairvoyants are normally able to see into the invisible world encountered by most only in altered states of consciousness.

4 The Principle of Polarity or Duality

Everything in nature is dual and polarised. This has already been noted in connection with the creative and constructive principles referred to in the etymology of the world paneurhythmy. Electricity works through positive and negative charges, while magnetism operates through two poles, applying not only to the Earth herself but also to crystals and eggs. Trees and plants are polarised into roots and branches or shoots.

The human physical body also expresses the creative and constructive principles corresponding respectively to positive and negative, masculine and feminine. Beinsa Douno explains that our bodies have a triple polarity of upper and lower, right and left, front and back. We receive positive electromagnetism through the right arm and leg, and negative electromagnetism through the left arm and leg; then we are able to expel superfluous energy behind us. These processes are especially exemplified in the exercises 'Ascending', 'Elevation' and 'Aoum'. This knowledge of polarity and the flow of energy during the exercises enables one better to direct one's thoughts and feelings, thus making the gestures conscious and not merely mechanical. The polarisation also explains why almost every exercise begins on the right, creative foot and continues with the left, constructive one; alternation of the feet produces an exchange between positive and negative currents. The exercises themselves are danced in pairs, which exchange energy between them in such movements as 'Weaving', 'Acquaintance' and 'Beautiful Day'.

The dancer will find a great variety of movements in the exercises, for instance straight lines, curves and wave motions. The lines predominate in the strong exercises like 'Conquering' and 'Elevation', while the curves are more evident in 'Reconciliation' and 'Joy of the Earth'. Quite frequently one finds these polarities in successive exercises, making the contrasting feel extremely distinct.

5 The Principle of Rhythm

We have already mentioned rhythm or periodicity in discussing the etymology of paneurhythmy. Our lives revolve round the cycles and rhythms of day and night, life and death, inhalation and exhalation, creation and destruction, Spring and Autumn, Summer and Winter. There are rhythms in the orbits of planets and comets, and even in the rise and decay of human cultures. We have rhythms or habits in our daily lives, in our biological cycles. Work is easier and more harmonious if we introduce rhythm into it. Beinsa Douno even explains that there is a correspondence between the rhythm of solar rays and the rhythm of the heart.

Each paneurhythmy exercise has its own definite rhythm, which is often transparently linked to the idea and music: in 'Liberation', the downbeat corresponds to the gesture of liberation from chains, while in 'Jumping' it is as if one coils up like a spring before releasing the tension in the jump itself, the last two notes of which represent the leap in the air and the landing on the ground.

6 The Principle of Cause and Effect

This link is the basis of logical coherence in space-time. It also underpins the analysis of the effects of the paneurhythmy exercises to be outlined in the next section.

7 The Principle of Unity or Relatedness

Everything in nature is related through a basis of unity, which we also saw illustrated in the Correspondence Principle explained above, especially in relation to the elements being different combinations of the same electrons. This principle is clearly demonstrated in the dancing of the paneurhythmy itself and the corresponding relatedness of the dancers to each other and to the whole. We are also parts of the Whole in a more general sense; individuals in relation to the whole human race like the cells of our bodies, separate but part of the whole. This insight lies at the basis of Beinsa Douno's political ideas of the part living for the whole through loving service. Dancing the paneurhythmy together is a prototype of a more advanced kind of human cooperation. It harmonises our individual and collective energy.

EFFECTS

The effects of practising the paneurhythmy could be deduced from some of the principles outlined above, which could be summarised as follows:

(1) The reciprocity between human beings and Nature.
(2) The correlation between human physiological and psychological processes.
(3) The relationship between thought, music and movement.

The full benefits of paneurhythmy can only be achieved by participating with one's whole being at all levels: physical, spiritual and Divine as body, soul and Spirit; and in the psycho-physiological realm through the action of mind, heart and will. Mechanical performance of the exercises will only produce basic physical benefits achievable by ordinary forms of exercise.

Beinsa Douno insists that the fundamental idea which should pervade our consciousness during the execution of the exercises is the idea of God; of what is eternal and majestic; of supreme Wisdom. A corresponding thought is the rising of the sun (one of the exercises) which itself is correlated with the awakening of the human soul: the human soul aspires towards the sun as the bearer of health and strength.

It is important to realise that we operate as transmitters and receivers of energy, thoughts and feelings, especially in view of the nature of paneurhythmy as an exchange between human beings and Nature (there is also an exchange with the Divine world and with each other). During the exercises we can both give out and receive. In 'Giving', for example, we send out the impulse of giving through the performance of the movement with its corresponding idea and music; in 'Aoum' we effect a transmission and exchange between solar and terrestrial energy through our hands. All this stresses the importance of directing one's thoughts and feelings into one's hands and feet at the right moment. Beinsa Douno explains that, in accordance with the polarities of the body explained in the last section, the dancer should direct the thoughts and feelings as follows: when you stretch out your right hand in front and your left hand behind (see 'Ascending', 'Elevation', 'Aoum' and 'Beauty', for instance) you should project your mind into your right hand and your heart into your left; similarly, when you move your right foot, you project the mind into it and your heart into the left. In this way we become living transmitters of divine ideas: these forces of renewal are manifest through us.

One level of the effects of practising the paneurhythmy is purely physical. The variety of exercise strengthens the organism and the muscles; it improves breathing and blood circulation and, if performed in the early morning, makes the nervous system more resilient through the beneficial effects of the sun's rays. Beinsa Douno also gave many other gymnastic exercises to maintain the health and suppleness of the physical system. A different effect is produced by the exercises using curved lines, namely an enhancement of one's natural fluidity and harmony of movement.

A second level of effects stems from the fact that the movements themselves are the fruit of a perfect knowledge of the living energies of nature and the forces which are latent and active in the human being; they act as a stimulant towards the development of our potential. The three effects here are described as follows:

(1) The exercises are energy accumulators through which we are linked to the creative and constructive forces of nature: we receive this life-giving energy which contributes to the unfolding of our potential.

(2) As the paneurhythmy movements are in harmony with the cosmic rhythm which animates the whole of life, they activate all the latent forces of the human soul and impel them towards action. This awakening is just the opening of the bud, after which comes the blossom and the fruit.

(3) The nature of these exercises means that the dancer transmits thoughts, ideas and forces into the world at large which continue to work for its renewal. The hands are particularly important in this respect, as Beinsa Douno explains that they emit beams of light, slightly different according to the character of each finger and the links of the three parts of the finger with the three worlds – physical, spiritual and Divine. The hands represent lines of force along which flows the living energy which can put us in touch with the living forces of nature.

A third level of effects is more specifically concerned with the development of our spiritual capacities through the mind and the brain. In human beings the Divine Logos is able to work consciously from the inside, not simply unconsciously as in the other Kingdoms. It is well known that there are areas in the motor cortex of the brain which are linked to the movement of various limbs; thus movement of a limb is correlated with increased cerebral blood flow to a particular area of this cortex. The parts of the brain are linked respectively to a higher spiritual world, to spiritual capacities, and to certain organs in the body. We shall look at each in turn.

1. Link with higher worlds

A particular movement stimulates a part of the brain which in turn is linked with a world of advanced beings. Beinsa Douno explains that we are surrounded by a world of noetic beings, and therefore by their thoughts, energy and life. We should try to become conscious of this fact. Some of these beings have already finished their evolution and have therefore proceeded further along the path of development than we have. It is a path of ascent and illumination. These beings work harmoniously with the cosmic rhythm and exist in a world of supreme beauty and order. If we tune ourselves to their world, they can transmit to us their ideas, impulses, strength and light. When we are inspired or enlightened by great ideas, it is a gift from these beings; we have received something of their clear thoughts and prophetic vision of our spiritual evolution.

2. Link with spiritual faculties

Frequent and conscious practice of the paneurhythmy exercises will stimulate the development of certain parts of the motor cortex which, Beinsa Douno explains, correspond to higher spiritual faculties like mercy, love, faith and hope, or to mental capacities or sensitivity to music. The stimulation of these parts awakens and develops our spiritual gifts. A refinement of the nervous system also puts us in resonance with the higher divine ideas of which the movements themselves are the true expression.

3. Link with physical organs

The correspondence here stimulates the operation of particular organs in the body, strengthening them, increasing their capacity and regularising their function. No details have been given here, but the dancer can develop a sensitivity to these and other effects of the exercises.

All the effects of paneurhythmy are transformative and ennobling. One's physical, emotional, mental and spiritual health is enhanced, as is one's general sense of harmony and music through ear and gesture. The exercises contribute not only to our own evolution but also, as we shall see below, to the evolution of the human race.

THE RENEWAL OF CULTURE

The publication in 1917 of Oswald Spengler's *Decline of the West* marked an important advance in the comparative study of cultures, an enterprise taken a good deal further by Arnold Toynbee in his monumental *Study of History*. While Spengler's approach is mechanical, Toynbee adopts a more organic perspective in seeking parallels in the rise and decline of cultures. Beinsa Douno's philosophy of history sees humankind moving from a culture based on objective knowledge to one based on love and fraternity. This conception goes far beyond external manipulation through genetic engineering, since nothing really changes if the mentality and outlook on life remains the same. What is required, according to Beinsa Douno, is a new conception of Life and attitude towards our problems.

Present-day culture he regarded as a chaotic transition phase between two cultures, where the old is in the process of disintegrating and the new is as yet still in bud. The key feature of the emerging culture is an extension of consciousness and sympathy, the awakening of Cosmic Consciousness 'where people will raise themselves above personal concerns and will enter the unlimited and universal life of the Whole'. The new spirit approaching is that of fraternity and unity, of which paneurhythmy is the outer form and expression in accordance with the principles of correspondence already discussed.

Beinsa Douno prophesies the advent of a new epoch representing the Cosmic Spring, a solar culture in which, symbolically, the ice and snow will melt, the flowers bloom, and the birds arrive from the south. It is early days as yet: the whole process will probably take decades. In any event, paneurhythmy is both a preparation for and an expression of this new culture. When we dance the paneurhythmy, we transmit the ideas of the new culture which are contained in the movements, thus setting up a resonance and energy flow of renewal. The living circle of the paneurhythmy creates and constructs Divine qualities within the dancers at the same time as sending out their impulse into the world. It is a contribution to the creation of a new world order.

It is explained that 'all the new ideas which are to be part of this new culture, all the vital principles of renewal and which have the inner power to raise humanity to the level of this new life are contained in the exercises'. The forces of the rising culture are detailed as follows:

1. Goodness
This is the rock, the solid foundation of any kind of sacred and noetic life. Whatever is built on goodness is indestructible. What can be destroyed is not good. Goodness links human beings to an inexhaustible source of strength. The strength of goodness makes a person as solid as a rock in the face of every difficulty and obstacle, strong enough to sustain and overcome everything.

2. Justice
This is the just distribution of light, heat, power and all the goods so generously provided by nature. They are a gift for all. Every being which comes to earth has a right to life, sun and all other essentials. Justice is a precondition of normal growth and prosperity. It brings the conditions for growth. Only where justice reigns can there be normal growth, natural development and spiritual upliftment.

3. Higher noetic reason

This implies the orderly use, with a specific end in view, of light, heat, energy and other goods. Only in the realm of the Noetic is there fruit; and only there does fruit ripen. In other words, only in the realm of the Noetic are there lasting and beneficial results. The higher reason includes the Great Wisdom, the Great Knowledge which reveal the forces, laws and methods of work. This is the deep understanding of nature, humanity and life. The Noetic is an expression of a harmonious combination of Love and Wisdom.

4. Harmony

When all the strings of an instrument are harmoniously attuned, they can produce beautiful melodies. Only by means of such an instrument can a virtuoso player show his talent and power of performance. In the same way, when the instruments of an orchestra are attuned to each other, the conductor can raise his baton and express through it the great idea which enlightens and inspires him.

All beings represent a great cosmic orchestra. When harmony reigns among them, the great Conductor can express through this orchestra the music of the noetic life, as well as his own greatness, the beauty of his thought and his great love. The original goal of religion was the coordination of human beings with terrestrial and solar energy. Having lost sight of this goal, we think we can make people good, but how can this come about if they are not attuned? The violin must first be tuned before it can be beautifully played.

5. Fraternity

The culture of the fraternity of all peoples is approaching. They will all consider themselves as members of a great family. The stronger nations will help the weaker ones. All peoples are organs of the great cosmic organism, and as such have their assigned place, function and special mission. This idea is currently arising in the collective consciousness.

6. Freedom

Freedom is the removal of all barriers, limitations and obstacles which prevent the divine nature in human beings from manifesting in the world in its full beauty, splendour and scope. Freedom is the discovery of the great treasures buried in the human soul. In freedom, the soul takes charge. Freedom is the loosing of all chains, the collapse of narrow ideas and errors, and an entry into the boundless possibilities concealed within the human spirit.

Freedom is the opening of beautiful perspectives of upliftment and attainment.

7. Cosmic Love

In the course of its development, human consciousness is transformed into Love. Cosmic Love embraces all the above forces and bears them within itself. These forces are its expression. Today, Cosmic Love is coming to birth in human consiousness as a new insight into the essence of Life. This is an exit from death and an entry into Life; the leaving behind of the life of shadows and entry into the life of a majestic reality – the path towards the source of Life itself. It is what reconciles all contradictions and surmounts all difficulties. It is resurrection.

Only the person who is pure in body, mind and heart will understand the nature of human happiness and Cosmic Love. When people enter the realm of purity, through their hearts will flow the crystalline, life-giving currents of Cosmic Love.

In conclusion, Beinsa Douno states that paneurhythmy is a great force which will give a new inspiration to the world:

Paneurhythmy is the key of my Teaching which brings peace to human souls. They must receive this key from you; you must give it to them. It will open the souls still plunged in the world of oblivion. The consciousness of these beings will be illuminated, and they will grasp the meaning of their life. The great evolved Souls will implant in them the graft of Love; and this world, grafted from within, will acquire a new light and a new impulse towards all other aspirations: from involution to evolution; from unending wars towards eternal peace; from hatred towards Divine Love; from egotism towards self-abnegation.

NOTES

1. Much of this chapter is directly taken from a major lecture given by the Master on paneurhythmy in July 1943. I have tried to organise this and other material into a coherent and sequential whole.

CHAPTER FOUR

How to Perform the Paneurhythmy Exercises

THE CIRCLE

Paneurhythmy is danced in couples in a circle which moves anti-clockwise. Partners should be an arm's length away from each other and 1½ metres behind the preceding couple. Men usually dance on the outside. Unless otherwise stated, the exercises are naturally danced with the left shoulder facing the centre.

THE FIRST DAY OF SPRING

The first ten exercises are called 'The First Day of Spring' and follow directly on from each other without a break. They represent an introduction to the New Life, as in Spring, when an abundant flow of energy awakens the sleeping potential for growth in Nature. The words of the first movement speak of the first day of Spring as the first day of joy and love, bringing us strength and life. The same process occurs in our inner life when the soul awakens to a new life, a new awareness of the Divine.

1. AWAKENING

Description

Melody 1 is played twice, making 40 bars.

Starting position
All dancers face to the right, feet together. The hands are placed on the shoulders, fingers closed with the thumb on the index finger, forearms horizontal (figure 2).

Fig 2   Fig 3

Movements

(1) The right foot steps forward, and the arms simultaneously open and unfold in a circle to each side with the palms turning downward as they reach a horizontal position on either side of the body (figure 3).

Note: The Master first gave this exercise with the palms remaining upwards throughout the unfolding movement, but later modified it.

(2) The left foot steps forward and the hands are placed back on the shoulders, fingers closed as described above.

These movements are then repeated until the end of the 40 bars of music. On the last movement with the left foot, the hands are brought in front of the chest, palms downward, with thumb and index finger touching each other and ready for the second exercise.

Explanation

The initial position of this exercise, with the fingers closed and placed on the shoulders, indicates that the person is closed and contained within themselves. Like the grain of wheat sown in the field, we are awaiting the appropriate moment to break through the soil into the light, signifying the outgrowing of narrow and limited personal concerns as we enter into the wider realm of the Life of the Whole.

The first gesture is opening the arms to the sides, similar to the opening of a flower, a movement of giving which represents the creative masculine principle also symbolised by the stepping forward of the right foot. The first movement is thus giving out what we have within. When the hands and fingers stretch out, they act as emitters and receivers of energies: the fingers give out energy, while the gaps between the fingers receive it. It is important to keep the fingers straight and slightly apart throughout the exercises.

The second gesture, placing the hands back on the shoulders, is receiving from nature and represents the feminine principle of receiving and constructing.

These two gestures of giving and receiving, of exchange, are successive states. The idea of giving what one has received already implies a broadening of our personal context and represents the beginning of the full manifestation of the human soul. When this exercise is performed with an awakened consciousness, it implants this key idea of receiving and giving what one has received. This fruitful idea is actually sent out into the world through the energy of these movements: they therefore perform a dual function of implanting the idea within the dancers themselves and transmitting it into the world as a creative impulse.

2. RECONCILIATION

Melody 2 – 30 bars

Description

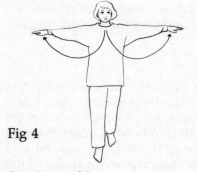

Fig 4   Fig 5

Starting position
The last movement of the previous exercise is the point of departure.

Movements
(1) The right foot steps forward and the hands simultaneously separate, describing a downward circle until they reach the horizontal position, with palms turned downwards (figure 4).

(2) The left foot steps forwards, and the arms return to a position in front of the chest, with hands together facing forwards and slightly upwards (figure 5).

These movements continue until the end of the 30 bars.
On the last bar, with the step of the left foot, the hands are brought onto the upper chest.

Explanation

The movements of this exercise are flowing curves representing the feminine principle. The coming together of the left and right hands is the reconciliation of positive and negative poles which brings about balance and harmony.

This exercise encourages us to resolve our difficulties through gentleness and reconciliation, qualities of the heart, rather than through force: 'Gentleness prepares the way of Love. It neither tramples on the crushed reed nor extinguishes the flickering lamp. It permeates the earth with the radiance of the Angelic World'.

3. GIVING

Melody 3 – 34 bars

Description

Fig 6

Starting position
The weight is on the right foot, with fingers placed on the chest and palms turned inwards.

Movements
(1) The right foot steps forward and the arms unfold to the front in a gesture of giving. They end parallel and horizontal, palms upward, fingers stretched out (figure 6).

(2) The left foot steps forward and the hands simultaneously return to their original position.

The alternating movements are continued until the 34th bar, when the hands are against the chest.

Explanation

The giving and receiving in this exercise express the exchange between the inner and outer life, and between ourselves and the Energies of Living Nature. What we receive from nature needs to be elaborated within and given out again. This exercise puts us in contact with the energy and abundance of nature. We realise that the more we give, the more we receive. If we are vases already full to the brim, we cannot take in anything else from the outside. As soon as the vase is empty, it can be filled once more. If it is not emptied, the same old content remains in it. We must therefore give what we have in order to receive anew.

This is a process of refreshment, renewal, growth, joy and strength. If the source does not constantly give out what it is sent, it will be unable to receive any fresh water and it will soon find itself turning into a stagnant marsh. What a difference there is between this and a living source! In the first case we encounter decomposition and death; while in the second, in a pure source, there is a movement of life.

These movements have a powerful influence on the human personal growth, since they send out a strong impulse of giving into the world. This leads to a profound understanding of the sublime idea of giving and receiving. These exercises are capable of giving birth to great ideals: they awaken the qualities which will be the basis of the approaching new culture, a culture of sacrifice which will often impel one to give out; this will be a culture of sacrifice and giving, of self-abnegation in favour of others.

4. ASCENDING

Melody 4 – 26 bars

Description

Starting position
As at end of previous movement.

Fig 7

Fig 8

Movements
(1) The right foot steps forward and simultaneously the right hand is extended forwards and upwards, with the palm down and fingers straight. At the same time, the left hand extends downwards and backwards to form a straight line with the right hand (figure 7).
(2) The left foot steps forward and the positions of hands and feet are reversed (figure 8).

These movements are repeated until the end of the melody. The effect is that of producing alternating semi-circular arcs.
On the last bar, both hands are lowered down the side of the body.

Explanation

These successive gestures of right and left hand express the eternal process of life in its rising and falling, like the movement of the tides. Descending symbolises the valley of suffering or poverty, while rising is the summit of joy and wealth. The raising and lowering of the arms is paralleled by that of the feet as we lift them and put them back on the ground. We need to accept and understand these processes as part of the natural order. We need to go down before we can go up again. Raising the right hand signifies an action of the mind, and the left hand an action of the heart.

When a soul awakens from the deep sleep of material life, she looks up towards the heights of the Spirit. The mountain is the emblem of the Divine World, a sacred place where the soul which has awakened to the

Divine Life aspires to rise so as to absorb the light and strength essential for the completion of her earthly journey. The act of climbing the mountain helps people to overcome the inertia of matter, to broaden the horizon of their thoughts and ideas, and to achieve purity of heart.

5. ELEVATION

Melody 5 – 26 bars

Description

Fig 9   Fig 10

Starting position
Arms lowered by the side, palms back, weight on the left foot.

Movements
(1) The right foot steps forward, while simultaneously both hands stretch forward and upward, palms to the front and fingers straight (figure 9).
(2) The left foot steps forward while both hands move downwards and backwards behind the body, fingers pointed down and hands facing back (figure 10). Two parallel descending and ascending arcs are described.

The movements continue until the end of the music. The preparation for the next movement consists of bringing the right hand in front of the chest, palm down, and placing the left hand on the waist; all this on the final left foot step.

Explanation

When we raise our arms together, we are receiving the light of the New Dawn coming from the Divine World. The movement of the arms down and back signifies that, having adopted the new, we put old ideas behind us. Raising both hands at the same time indicates the powerful joint action of mind and heart and expresses the energy which drives us onwards on the path of Life, just as the movement of oars pushes the boat along.

Elevation is the aspiration of the soul towards the beautiful and the sublime; it is also a call to all souls to enter on that path.

A sweet joy pervades the being. The vision of a hitherto unknown life comes into view. People have long felt a yearning for it and have always sought it; they are just now discovering the path of this life. There dawns in the soul a resolve to walk on this path and to abandon outworn ideas. New forces awaken within.

6. OPENING

Melody 6 – 40 bars

Description

Starting position

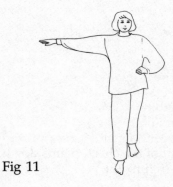

Fig 11

Fig 12

Left hand on hip, right hand in front of sternum, palm down; weight on left foot.

Movements
(1) The right foot steps forward while the right hand describes a horizontal circle and opens right out; the palm remains turned towards the ground (figure 11).
(2) The left foot steps forward and the right hand is brought back to the starting position (figure 12).
(3) At the beginning of the 19th bar the right foot steps forward and the hands change position – the right hand on the hip and the left in front of the chest.
(4) The left foot steps forward and the left hand describes the same circle as indicated above for the right hand.

At the final beat on the right foot, the hands are brought together in front of the chest in preparation for the next movement.

Explanation

These horizontal semi-circular arcs described by the right and left hands indicate the respective resolution of mental and emotional problems. The hands emit certain forces which disperse the obstacles along the bright path of the soul so that she can begin the process of elevation and refinement.

The movements demonstrate an opening and closing motion. Once we have entered into the new path, we need to close off from the old and leave it behind. The gate of the past must be shut, while that of the future needs to be opened. The opening is carried out in the present by our act of will. Opening and closing of doors also symbolises the correct way of drawing conclusions in the realms of thought and feeling.

7. LIBERATION

Melody 6 – 40 bars

Description

Starting position
The hands are held a few inches in front of the chest, palms down, fists touching. Weight on the left foot (figure 13).

Movements
(1) The right foot steps forward and the hands simultaneously open, push down and out in a gesture of throwing something

Fig 13   Fig 14

away until the horizontal position is reached, palms downwards and fingers apart (figure 14). The gesture is definite and forceful, quite unlike 'Reconciliation'. It tends to reinforce the will.

(2) The left foot steps forwards and the hands return to the starting position in front of the chest, fists clenched.

These movements are repeated until the end of the music and lead straight into the next exercise.

Explanation

The powerful gesture represents liberation from all obstacles which block the development of the soul; it breaks with the former life and the errors of the past, enabling us to adopt and embrace the new. The liquidation of karmic bonds opens up the possibility of the life of freedom.

The exercise is a pressing invitation to free oneself, to emerge from prison. It says to us: 'Leave the life of eternal setting and enter into the life of eternal rising. Drop the chains of death, and enter into Life and liberty. Come out of the dark caves of lovelessness and enter into the joy of Love'. A powerful impulse to this effect is transmitted into the world through this movement.

8. CLAPPING

Melody 6 – 40 bars

Description

Fig 15

Starting position

As at end of previous exercise – hands are horizontal outwards, palms down.

Movements
(1) The left foot steps forward and the hands swing up to clap lightly level with the face. They immediately part and continue their rising movement outwards again (figure 15).
(2) The right foot steps forward while the hands spread out to the horizontal, palms downward.

These movements continue until the end of the music. The next exercise continues straight on when, after the final clap, the hands are in front of the face.

Explanation

Clapping expresses the joy and triumph of freedom. The movements mean that we have freed ourselves from oppression and obstacles. They show the limits and beginnings of freedom, stating that it has been achieved.

The gesture is the joy of the soul which has acquired its freedom; the joy of the butterfly which has emerged from its cocoon; the joy of the flower opening up to the sun's rays for the first time.

9. PURIFICATION

Melody 9 (No. 1) – 40 bars

Description

Fig 16　　　　　　　　　　　　　　　　　　　　　　Fig 17

Starting position

The fingers are placed in front of the mouth, with the thumb, index and middle finger together; the other fingers are slightly open and curved, palms facing the front.

Movements
(1) The right foot steps forward and air is simultaneously blown through the fingers, which immediately open and spread outward to the sides until the arms are extended horizontally (figure 16). There is a slight downward curve in this movement.
(2) The left foot steps forward and the hands return to their original position (figure 17). The dancer breathes in.

The movements continue until the end of the music and lead straight on to the next exercise.

Explanation

The breath in this exercise signifies the Divine Word with its purifying qualities. To breathe in is to receive, and to breathe out to purify oneself. The opening movement of the arms is a gesture of sowing the seed of the Word: one receives the Word and sows it through the action of the tongue. The pure Word is introduced into life and thence into toughts, feelings and actions: 'May my thoughts be as luminous as the sun, and my feelings as pure as the water from mountain springs'.

'The life of disciples is extremely intense. They pass through the most profound joys and sufferings unknown to ordinary people. This is like the pain of all the seeds sown in the deep and dark earth. Once knowledge has been acquired, that is to say when the seed has been sown, the spiritual aspirant is subjected to the ordeal of isolation, silence and darkness; by means of these ordeals and in the struggle for survival, the soul is strengthened. The process of construction and alchemy is in its last phase, new energy flows in, bringing a creative impulse with it. That is the moment of incarnation, of birth, of return to life. A person's radiance and spiritual emanation depends on the intensity of their inner work'.

10. FLYING

Melody 10 (No. 2) – 30 bars

Description

Starting position
The hands extended with the weight on the right foot.

Movements
(1) The right foot steps forward and the arms make undulating movements imitating the flight of a bird. The movement is not just up and down, but incorporates a pushing out of the hands which effectively makes them describe a circle.
(2) The left foot steps forward while the same undulating motion is continued.

The movements continue until the end of the music, which marks the finish of the first cycle.

Explanation

These curved and undulating movements represent the wave motion of light, as well as the aspiration to rise so that everything may grow. What has been sown must grow. The Word must be propagated and sown in our lives. Having now acquired the strength to free ourselves from darkness, we return to life; 'such is the joy of every flower which has grown and entered the light'. At different levels Light encourages the growth of plants and that of human souls.

11. EVERA

Melody 11 – 68 bars

Description

Fig 18   Fig 19   Fig 20   Fig 21

Starting position

All dancers face the centre. Weight on the left foot with right foot
pointing to the right with only the toe on the ground. The right arm
is folded in front of the chest and the left arm extended to the left;
palms down, arms upwards at 45° (figure 18).

Movements
(1) Swivel to the right, shifting the weight onto the right foot,
simultaneously bringing the hands down in a semi-circle and up to
an angle of 45° to the right. Left foot is on the toe (figure 19).
(2) Turn 90° to the right, the left foot passing in front of the right;
at the same time, the hands push forward and up, parallel, with
palms facing each other (figure 20).
(3) Pivot 90° to the right, with the back facing the centre; the two
hands pass down in a semi-circle behind the body, palms
downwards. Left foot on its toe (figure 21).
(4) Movement 1 is repeated with the back facing the centre and the
gestures reversed.
(5) Reversed repeat of movement 2.
(6) Reversed repeat of movement 3.

This sequence is repeated until the end of the music. This is not an easy exercise to learn, and should first be practised in slow motion. The key thing is to count to three as the movements are executed; here the music is a great help.

Explanation

The movement is one of successive turning to the right and left while moving forwards. Here we have the action of the two principles of Love and Wisdom, the feminine and the masculine. When we turn inwards to the left we receive Love; when we turn outwards to the right, we receive Wisdom. The forward movement is towards the Truth. Thus the application of Love and Wisdom in our lives leads us towards the Truth. The advancing movement is the impulse towards growth and development.

> Universal Love created life, and Wisdom sustains it. These are the two principles which, when applied in life, help the raising of awareness in the world.
> The Truth in itself is something concrete, real and immutable. It is Eternal Light, Eternal Wisdom, Eternal Love, Eternal Justice, Eternal Life. If one embodies these five states one will truly understand the nature of Truth. Truth is the joint action of Love and Wisdom, it is the final outcome of Eternity.

This exercise helps us to deepen our understanding of the three cardinal principles of the Teaching of Beinsa Douno: Love, Wisdom and Truth.

12. JUMPING

Melody 12 – 15 bars

Description

Starting position
All dancers turn to face the centre. Hands above the head, palms forward (figure 22).

Movements
(1) During the playing of the first five notes, the dancers bend right down, bringing their arms down and behind, with palms upwards. The process is smooth and continuous (figure 23).

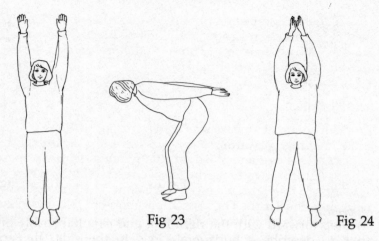

Fig 22   Fig 23   Fig 24

(2) The last two notes indicate the jump itself: unwind, jump in the air, and clap the hands together before returning to the starting position with palms facing forwards (figure 24).

These movements are repeated five times. At the end the hands should be brought down to the side of the body and one should make a turn to the right, feet together.

Explanation

Jumping represents the triumph of Love and Wisdom as they have been applied in life. First of all we bow before the Eternal, the Divine Principle working in the world. The jump is our offering and expression of joy to the Creator. There is a great spontaneity in this exercise, which puts one in contact again with the immediacy and joy of the child.

13. WEAVING

Melody 13 – 60 bars

Description

Starting position
Dancers are facing round the circle. The outside circle should make two paces in front of the inside. Palms in front of the sternum, facing down with middle fingers just touching. The elbows are horizontal (figure 25).

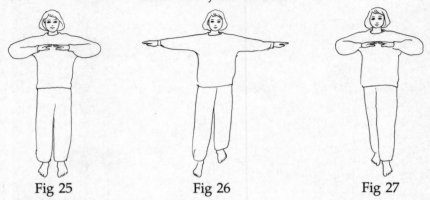

Fig 25   Fig 26   Fig 27

Movements
(1) Step forward with the right foot and simultaneously open the arms to describe a horizontal circle to the side; the arms are stretched right out with the palms still facing downwards (figure 26).
(2) Step forward with the left foot and bring the arms back to the starting position (as in figure 27).
(3) Repeat these movements four times. The last step with the left foot brings the feet together again. It is important to keep counting to eight in this exercise if one is not to lose time and direction.
(4) Crossing.
The arms continue to open and close as before. The outer circle partner always passes in front of the inner; thus the inner behind the outer.

Inner→Outer: step with the *left* foot crossing *over* the right and continue counting to eight while crossing behind, until the feet come together on the eighth movement.
Outer→Inner: Step with the *right* foot crossing *over* the left and continue counting to eight while crossing in front of your partner until feet come together at the eighth movement.

The positions of the two partners have now been reversed.
(5) Both partners go straight ahead for eight steps, repeating movements 1 to 3.
(6) Movement 4 – crossing – is repeated so that the partners revert to their original positions.
(7) At the end of the sequence the partners will find their positions reversed; these should be maintained for the rest of the paneurhythmy. The partners should be level with each other for the next exercise.

This exercise is quite straightforward if one keeps counting. It is also important for the inner circle to take small steps if the circle is small.

Explanation

This movement expresses the organic and constructive process in Nature, and makes us conscious of the interaction of polarities exemplified in the crossing pattern of the two partners. The parallel forward movement signifies that the rhythm and harmony received and elaborated by human beings should be reflected outwards and transmitted to the life of humanity and nature. At another level, as indicated by the words accompanying the music, the exercise is about the weaving of the most beautiful thoughts which can be poured into our souls as a pure and sacred life force so that peace and love, kindness and mercy should reign in our hearts. Every day we work and grow, sowing the seeds of good about us.

14. THINKING

Melody 13 – 60 bars

Description

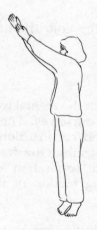

Fig 28   Fig 29

Starting position
Arms are held diagonally up to the right at 45°, fingers outstretched, palms facing each other (figure 28).

Movements
(1) The hands swing down in a semi-circular movement towards the left and up to the corresponding 45° angle on the left; feet remain stationary. During this process one sings *'Misli!'* (Think!)
(2) The hands swing down and back up to the starting position, during which one sings *'Pravo misli'* (Think justly and correctly!)
(3) Movements 1 and 2 are repeated.
(4) The partners then take 24 steps forward (6 × 4), starting with the right foot. On each step one makes a circular movement with the hands as if to surround a sphere, starting from the top (palms down). When the hands meet at the bottom (palms up), the hands go up through the middle to start the next sphere (figure 29). During this movement one sings *'Sveshdeni misli za jivota ti krepi'* (Sustain your life with sacred thoughts) four times in accordance with the music. It is best to learn this song separately before incorporating it into the movements.
(5) One continues walking as the music changes and one stretches the hands out sideways as if to support something – palms outwards, fingers pointing up. One sings *'Krepi!'* (Sustain!) with each push.
(6) Movement 4 resumes for 7 paces as one repeats *'Sveshdeni misli za jivota ti krepi'* once.
(7) Movement 5 is exactly repeated with the *'Krepi'*.
(8) Identical to 6, that is, one more round.

The entire exercise is then repeated. At the end, the hands are brought down to the sides.

Explanation

The first part of the exercise connects us with the mental world and elevated thoughts: we receive these into ourselves. The circular movements represent the assimilation and construction of this energy of Just Thought; the gesture also resembles the drawing up of water. Finally, the maintenance and application of these thoughts is symbolised by the supporting motion of the third movement.

> Human strength lies in what is sustained in the core of our being, sacred thoughts concerning the whole of life. If we nurture such thoughts, they will sustain us in all circumstances; if we abandon them, we are heading for a fall.

Thought based on Love is just and unlimited. In the absence of Love, thought cannot develop properly. Love is the initial impulse of human thought.

The person who entertains pure thoughts is freed from worries and anxieties. Just Thought brings joy and enables us to see the bright side of life.

You receive into yourself what you are thinking about. Dwell on Truth, Love, Wisdom, Equity and Virtue, and they will dwell within you. The water which comes out of the depths is pure.

15. AOUM

Melody 15 – 32 bars, singing 'Aoum, Aoum, Aoum, Om, Om, Aoumen'.

Description

Starting position
Feet together, hands at the sides.

Movements
(1) The right foot steps forward. Simultaneously, the right hand and arm extend forward and upward at a 45° angle, while the left arm extends downward in the opposite direction. The left leg is held straight backward, and the toe is lifted and pointed at the end of the movement (figure 30). The word 'Aoum' is sung.

Fig 30

(2) The left foot steps forward and the movements are inverted; 'Aoum' is sung again.

These movements alternate so that (1) is performed four times and (2) three times. The last Aoumen takes two movements. The second sequence then begins on the left foot.

Explanation

There is a current coming from the sun which passes through the centre of the earth, and another current coming from the earth which passes through the sun. In this exercise, when the arm is extended forward and up at 45°, it receives the energies coming from the Divine Centre. Through the foot placed on the ground we receive the telluric energies coming from the centre of the earth. Through the foot and hand stretched backwards we expel impure and disharmonious energy into the earth.

The successive movements of the arms forwards and upwards represent the eternal aspiration of the human spirit towards the sublime heights. We live and work on the earth, but our inner gaze is always linked to the Divine which it seeks to express outwardly in the physical domain. The exercise links the polarities of spirit and matter, above and below.

Aoum is taken from an ancient Sacred Song, composed in the minor key, and which I have transposed into the major. As it stood – in the minor key – you would not have been able to withstand the vibrations, which would have risked altering your heartbeat.

When people sing Sacred Songs or practise Sacred Exercises, they should open their souls like a flower opening to the light. They should place themselves in a receptive and innocent state, like a pure and contented child who has no fears. People who reach this state will be at one with the Universal Forces.

People should regard this exercise as sacred:
'Aoum' is the expression of the Spirit.
'Aoum' is the Universal Spirit.
'Aoum' is the Universal Soul.

During this exercise one can think of the following formula of the Master:
God reigns in Heaven
God reigns on Earth
Blessed be His Name

16. THE RISING SUN

Melody 16 – 82 bars. The exercise is danced twice, and consists of three sequences which follow on immediately from each other.

Description

Starting position
Feet together, arms into the chest, palms down, fingers touching lightly (figure 31).

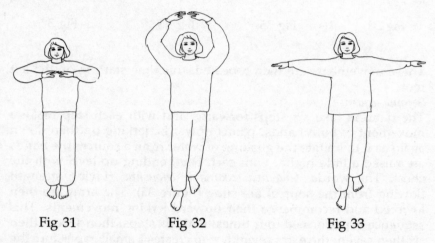

Fig 31   Fig 32   Fig 33

Movements

First sequence
(1) The right foot steps forward, while the hands are raised slowly above the head to form a semi-circle with middle fingers lightly touching (figure 32). The words *'Izgreva sleunceto'* (The sun is rising) are sung.
(2) The left foot steps forward with the right foot remaining on the toe. At the same time, the hands above the head turn palms outwards and describe a descending semi-circle, ending horizontal with the palms down (figure 33). The words *'Prashta svetlina'* (spreading its light) are sung.
(3) The right foot steps forward, with the left remaining on its toe. The hands are turned to face the front and are slowly brought back together onto the chest, palms inwards (figure 34). The words *'nossi radost za jivota tia'* (bringing joy to everything alive) are sung.

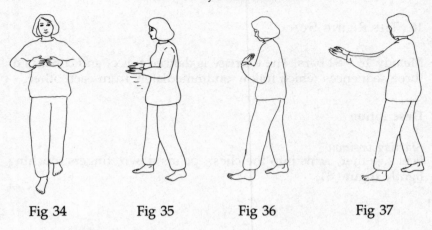

Fig 34   Fig 35   Fig 36   Fig 37

These movements are then repeated, this time starting on the left foot.

Second sequence

The dancers take six steps forwards and with each step make a movement of both hands, palms upwards, jerking up then down again as if to imitate the gushing of water from a source; the hands are raised a little higher with each beat, ending up level with the chest. The words '*Cila jiva izvorna te choushta*' (Living strength flowing from the source) are sung (figure 35). The arms are then lowered and recommence their upward jerking movements. This sequence is performed four times: with six steps, then seven, then six then seven; the extra seventh step creates a small gap before the arm movements resume. This sequence finishes on the left foot and leads directly into the *third sequence*.

(1) Step forward with the right foot and bring the hands into the chest, palms inwards and facing upwards (figure 36).

(2) Step forward with the left foot and extend the arms as in 'Giving' (Exercise 3) (figure 37).

As the dancers step forward they sing '*Zoun me zoun, zoun me zoun, bi-nom tometo*' twice (a phrase from the Vatan language affirming that the aspiration be fulfilled). The last ten steps are repeated before the whole of the three sequences is performed again.

Explanation

The meeting of the sunrise is an integral part of the mountain camps, and is one of the most sacred and precious moments of the day. The first sequence recreates the rising of the sun in gestures and words: the first movement expresses the emergence of the sun above the horizon, the second the spreading of its light, and the third its gift of life and joy: the arms move successively up, out in a semi-circle and back into the chest. The sequence as a whole represents the birth of a new conception of life.

The second sequence, imitating the bubbling up of a spring, signifies the upsurge of energy through the body. The rising movements are always greater than the descending ones. 'The tones of this melody express the movement of water gushing from a spring, both upwards and outwards. Suppressed energies are liberated and redirected.'

The third sequence represents the gestures of giving and receiving from the heart: the energy purified by the source should be distributed.

In order to perform this exercise correctly, people should be in harmonious contact with Divine Nature and with the Evolved Beings of the Invisible World, intelligence, devotion, gentleness. By listening to their voice in the depths of our being, we will remain on the true Path and will not be waylaid.

Human happiness consists of giving out to others the best in oneself. The rising sun is a Living Centre towards which the thought of great noetic beings is directed.

17. SQUARE

Melody 17 – 64 bars

Description

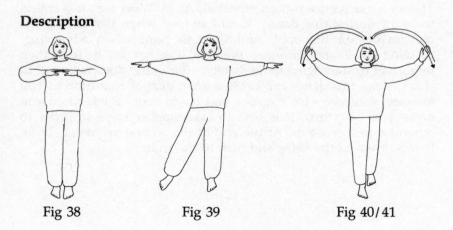

Fig 38   Fig 39   Fig 40/41

Starting position
Dancers face the centre with feet together. Arms and elbows are horizontal, hands in front of the chest, palms down, middle fingers touching (figure 38).

Movements
(1) The right foot steps to the side and taps the ground lightly. At the same time, the hands spread out horizontally to the sides, palms down (figure 39).
(2) The right foot and hands return to the starting position.
(3) Movement 1 is repeated with the left foot.
(4) Movement 2 is repeated, the left foot and the hands returning to the starting position.
(5) Repeat these four movements.
(6) The right foot steps forward towards the centre. Simultaneously the palms turn outward towards the front and sweep up and round to describe two semi-circles, descending to the horizontal position (figures 40 and 41).
(7) The left foot steps forward and the hands retrace their path back to the starting position, with palms horizontally below the chin and facing forwards.
(8) Movements 5 and 6 are done for 8 steps, but on the 7th step the right foot turns 90° to the left, and on the 8th step the left foot is placed next to the right. The hands return to their starting position in front of the chest.
(9) In this position (right shoulder facing the centre), movements 1 to 8 are repeated. After the 90° turn, the dancers will have their backs to the centre. The dance is repeated until, after the fourth round, all dancers have completed a square and are once again facing the centre.
The whole sequence is then repeated. As in 'Weaving', it is critical to count during this dance. Count to four when performing the movements on the spot, and then to eight when advancing, pivoting on 7 and bringing the feet together on 8. It is then important to start again immediately – the music does not wait! In small circles this dance can cause a great deal of confusion as you intersect someone else's square and try to avoid them when you make your 90° turn. It is best to take smaller steps in order to minimise this problem. At the end of the second sequence, bring hands down to the sides and turn to the right.

Explanation

This exercise is about the elaboration of a just and harmonious conception of how to use the goods of earthly life. The dancers turn successively towards the four cardinal points, thus linking themselves with their respective influences:

Turning towards the east signifies a link with the forces of Divine Justice

Towards the south links with the forces of Virtue

Towards the north links with the forces of Truth

Towards the west links with life on earth.

Facing west enables us to comprehend the value of the dynamic forces of Virtue, Divine Justice and Truth: how precious these forces are for us. It is when the sun has set that we realise how great a benefit it was to us; in the same way, we often only truly appreciate what we have lost.

> The essence of Man strives towards the good. The disciple, in the process of initiatic self-education, must cultivate good within. That is our earthly mission.
> The outer manifestation of Love is the good.
> Good lies in the accomplishment of the will of God.
> Good is all that unifies people, what is in harmony with the law of unity.
> The Law of Good states: 'Act towards your fellow human beings as the Creator acts towards you'.
> Good is a dynamic force which is working actively in the universe. If you do not link yourself in to this force, you will never be able to absorb its content.

The potential of the forces contained in 'Square' is elaborated in the two exercises which follow: 'Beauty' and 'Mobility'. It is significant that the symbolism of the square is that of contradictions. In a sermon in 1927, the Master drew a square and then two diagonals across it, making four triangles. The triangles, symbolising Love, Wisdom and Truth, are the solution to the contradictions.

18. BEAUTY

Melody 18 – 90 bars

Description

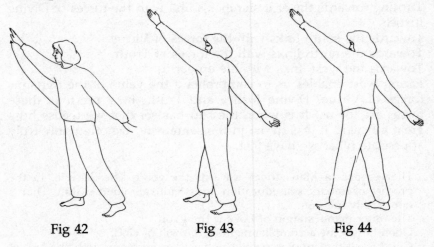

Fig 42   Fig 43   Fig 44

Starting position
As normal, hands by the side.

Movements
(1) The right foot steps forward and takes the weight, the left foot just leaving the ground; at the same time the right hand is projected forwards and up, palm to the front, and the left hand stretches backwards in a straight line with the right, palm back (figure 42). The weight is then transferred back onto the left foot, and foward again onto the right (figure 43).
(2) The left foot steps forward as the weight pivots onto the left foot, then back to the right and forward again onto the left. The left and right hands are projected forwards and backwards, inversely to movement 1 (figure 44).
These movements alternate until the end of the music. In this exercise the hands reach up towards the front in the smoothest way and there is a lightness of touch in the pivoting forwards and backwards. The rhythm is a counting to three.

Explanation

These movements represent the elaboration of the forces of 'Square' in an artistic fashion. The lines of movement are straight rather than curved – hence it is the masculine principle acting: light stimulating the action of thought so that we aspire to build a noble and decisive character.

> If we know how to recognise all the beauty which surrounds us, our souls will overflow with love for the greatness of the Unlimited, the Eternal.
> No earthly language or writing can describe the beauty of the Divine World. Only the saint and the being whose heart is filled with pure Love can raise their consciousness to the level of the Divine World and fill their soul with joy by contemplating the ineffable beauty which reigns there.

The more a being rises spiritually, the more they manifest the Divine within; the form of their body, the lines of their face become finer, more symmetrical, more harmonious. On the other hand, the people who, through their way of thinking and life, distances themselves from the Divine, from the higher and purer part of themselves, allow brutishness and lower forces to preponderate. Their faces lose their beauty and can even become ugly.

19. FLEXIBILITY

Melody 19 – 90 bars

Description

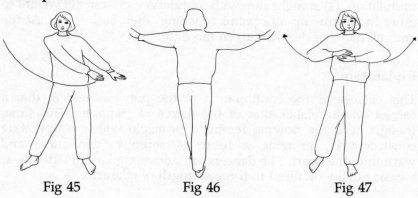

Fig 45   Fig 46   Fig 47

Starting position
All dancers face the centre. The body weight falls on the left foot, the right foot being pointed on its toe to the right. Hands are held down to the left at an angle of 45°, with the palms down (figure 45).

Movements
(1) The hands swing through in a semi-circle to the right, palms down, with the body weight moving to the right foot. The body turns slightly to the right.
(2) Continuing movement 1, the body pivots 180° to the right on the right toe, with the left foot making a semi-circle. The back is now facing the centre, the left foot in front. As soon as the pivot is complete, the right hand strokes the upper left palm before the arms spread out horizontally and perform an undulating motion by flexing at the wrists and elbows (as in 'Flying') (figure 46).
(3) The right foot steps forward and crosses over the left; the arms continue the undulating motion.
(4) The left foot steps to the left; undulation continues.
(5) The weight of the body is transferred to the right foot, the left remaining on its toe. At the same time, the right palm is placed on top of the left while the arms move back and up (figure 47).
(6) The right hand then strokes the left palm while the body weight is moved to the left foot and the body turns through 180°. A complete circle has now been made.
(7) The whole sequence of movements 1 to 6 is now repeated but inverted.
These movements alternate until the end of the music. This is not an easy exercise to master, and needs careful rehearsal in slow motion. Once again, counting can be a great help: (1) arms swing down, (2) pivot and brush palm, (3) crossover step with undulation, (4) straight step with undulation, (5) transfer weight to other foot, arms up and palms touching, then back to (1). At the end, all dancers should turn to the right.

Explanation

This exercise is the continuation of the previous one in that it carries on the elaboration of the forces of 'Square'. This time, though, it is the flowing feminine principle which is operating constructively, bringing a sense of serenity, gentleness and warmth to the heart. The dancers are cultivating kind-heartedness, a basic quality required to forge strength of character.

In this exercise, the right hand is transmitting positive magnetism, and the left hand negative magnetism. In the first brushing movement, the left hand is turned upwards to receive, the right downwards to give. The right palm first brushes the other palm, then the upper part of the left hand when it is facing downwards. Together with the pivoting motion, positive and negative currents are exchanged between the two sides of the body, producing a pleasant and energising sensation in the whole organism.

The lateral steps which follow, with the arms spread horizontally to the sides, represents the process of distributing the harmony created through the interaction of the two magnetic currents of the feminine principle.

In this way the elaboration of the potential forces of 'Square' is completed.

20. Conquering

Melody 20 – 80 bars

Description

| Fig 48 | Fig 49 | Fig 50 |

Starting position
Left shoulder towards the centre, weight on the right foot. Right hand down to the right of the right side at 45°, left hand across the front and parallel to the right. Palms back (figure 48).

Movements
(1) The hands swing forwards and upwards.
(2) The hands, still parallel, push straight up and to the front. At the same time, the right foot steps forward, while the left remains in place on the toe (figure 49).
(3) The hands move downwards behind and to the left. Body weight falls back onto the left foot while the right foot bends at the knee in preparation for the next step (figure 50).
(4) The body pivots forward again as in movement 1.
(5) The hands push up as the left foot steps forward, as in movement 2.
(6) As in movement 3, but reversed.
These movements are then repeated until the end of the music. Counting to three makes mastery of the movements easier. This exercise is similar to 'Evera', but with the critical difference that the torso must always be facing forwards when the arms are swinging to the side.

Explanation

This exercise represents, on the one hand, mastery of what has been acquired, and on the other, the feeling of veneration towards the Creator. The music and movements are definite and firm, expressing mastery of the knowledge and experience obtained so far. The pivoting back of the foot and the slight bow which accompanies it signify our reverence and gratitude towards the Creator for our gifts and capacities. This also indicates that we take time to reflect to gather the strength which will enable us to advance with renewed inspiration and commitment.

The words of this exercise clearly indicate its meaning:

> The day follows on from the night
> and joy succeeds sadness.
> We walk on a luminous path.
> No barrier stops us.
> We walk on and on
> our hearts filled with faith and love;
> we will fly towards victory,
> until our eyes gaze upon it.
> Valiantly we will look up,
> and walk boldly on,
> even in distress and unhappiness,
> for us, the world which God has created is
> beautiful.

We are caressed by a gentle south wind,
the birds are merrily singing.
In the morning, at sunrise,
we feel a nectar flowing in our souls.

Life consists of a constant renewal and work on oneself in order to acquire health, harmonious relations with others, knowledge and wisdom, generosity and love, and thus obtain a measure of happiness. Happiness is what we hold in our hands, that is what we have acquired through an effort of will.

Those who promise fulfilment without our acquiring such qualities are not telling the Truth.

21. JOY OF THE EARTH

Melody 21 – 80 bars

Description

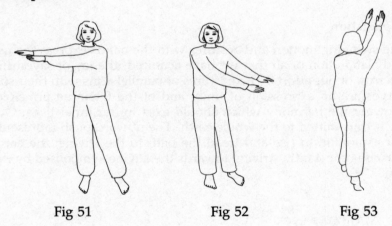

Fig 51   Fig 52   Fig 53

Starting position
All dancers face the centre, body weight on the right foot, the left foot pointed on the toe; hands parallel and horizontal to the right, palms down (figure 51).

Movements
(1) Pivot body weight to the left and simultaneously swing the arms down to the left in a semi-circle, with the right foot moving towards the left (figure 52).

(2) The right foot swings back to the right, and body weight swings back onto the right foot. At the same time, the arms swing back to the right side and the left foot gently lifts and moves towards the right one.

(3) Movements 1 and 2 are repeated.

(4) Pivot 90° to the right on the right foot and simultaneously swing the arms up to the right; the left foot steps forward, while the right one remains in place on the toe. At the same time, the arms push forwards and upwards 45° with a little push, as in 'Evera' (figure 53).

(5) Now pivot 90° to the right so that the back is facing towards the centre. The arms swing to the right and movements 1 to 4 are repeated but in reverse: one pivots to the left and steps forward with the right foot.

These movements alternate until the end of the music. The rhythm and movements here are very flowing, graceful and supple after the assertiveness of 'Conquering'. At the end of the exercise, brings hands down to the side and feet together.

Explanation

The swinging motion and gestures with the hands express the use and elaboration of all that we have acquired, the joy of savouring the fruit of our efforts. The gestures of parallel arms with their soft curves are an expression of unity and of the feminine principle, showing the harmony which should exist in our inner lives. Our joy is transmitted to the whole earth. The upward push represents our aspiration to rise and tread the path to the Divine; the earth herself is constantly striving towards the Divine symbolised by the sun.

22. ACQUAINTANCE

Melody 22 – 120 bars

Description

Starting position
Partners in the inner and outer circles turn and face each other, holding hands as follows: the inner partner holds the right hand up

at face level, and the left level with the solar plexus, while the outer circle partner is vice-versa. The right palm (acting-giving) is always above the left palm (passive-receiving) of the other dancer. Body weight falls on the right foot for the inner circle partner with the right hand up, and on the left foot for the outer circle partner with left hand up (figure 54). Feet slightly apart.

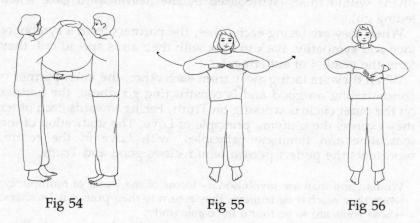

Fig 54　　　　　Fig 55　　　　　Fig 56

Movements

(1) The hands swing down, then partners let go and make a full turn so that they are back to back. Middle fingers touch, palms down, before the arms are spread out horizontally (figure 55). The pivot is done on the front foot, the weight now resting on the other foot following the turn.

(2) Dancers bring down their right hand to the left and grasp the fingers of the left hand; no movement of the feet (figure 56).

(4) The partners now pivot round to face each other once more, hands separate again and feet advance one pace (after the pivot). Partners catch each others' hands and the movements begin again.

(5) The body weight moves to the back foot; hands swing up and back with body weight moving appropriately. Partners once again let go and pivot 180°, as in Movement 1.

(6) These movements continue until the end of the music. Inside and outside circle movements mirror each other.

This is not an easy exercise to learn. I have tried to keep instructions simple. The swinging rhythm of the music helps coordinate the movements. As one holds one's partner's hands, one should look them in the eye, and then glance heavenwards just as one lets them go.

Explanation

There is an alternation here of holding hands and facing each other with letting go and being back to back. This represents the development of self-consciousness. It also expresses that we should appreciate the soul of others, seeing only what is good and divine within them (symbolised by the heavenward gaze when letting go).

When they are facing each other, the partners form a symbol of love and sympathy. Back to back with their arms spread out, they form the symbol of suffering.

When they are facing away from each other, the inner partner is concentrating on good and is constructing goodness; the partner on the outer circle is working on Truth. Facing towards each other they express the unifying principle of Love. The unification of the masculine and feminine principles, with Love in the centre, represents the perfect person who realises good and Truth.

> Woman and man are involutionary forms of the world of multiplicity; when they reach their fruition, they return to their primordial sources, whose roots are to be found in cosmic unity.
> May your look be gentle and pure, always animated by a divine thought.
> When two souls on earth love each other,
> The angels in Heaven sing.

23. BEAUTIFUL DAY

Melody 23 – 120 bars

Description

Starting position
As normal, hands on hips, feet together. Although there is considerable variation in the hand movements, the feet are regular throughout.

Movements
(1) The right leg is extended forward in the air as the left leg bends at the knee four times; the fourth time the right foot steps forward (figure 57).

Fig 57   Fig 58

(2) The same movement is repeated with reversed legs; the left foot steps forward this time.

Movements 1 and 2 are performed four times (32 bars).

(3) Repeat movement 1, but with right hand held forward and up, palm facing forwards (figure 58). Left hand is still on hip.

(4) Repeat movement 2, but with left hand up (right on hip).

Movements 3 and 4 are performed three times (24 bars). On the last movement, both hands return to the hips.

(5) Repeat movement 1, but this time the partners hold each other by the inside hands at shoulder level: the inner partner holds the right palm downward, and the outer holds the left palm upward (giving-receiving) (figure 59). The outer hand remains on the hips.

(6) Still holding hands, movement 2 is repeated.

Movements 5 and 6 are done four times (32 bars).

Fig 59

Fig 60

(7) Movement 1 is repeated with the partners' outside hands held high grasping each other, making an arc, while the inside hands hang free at the side; this time it is the outer partner whose right palm faces down, and the inner partner's left palm faces upwards to receive. The arm describes an arc on the way down as well (figure 60).

(8) Movement 2 is repeated with inside hands grasping as in movements 5 and 6; the outside hands hang free at the sides.

Movements 7 and 8 are repeated until the end of the music.

Explanation

This exercise is designed to strengthen the nervous system and stimulate the will. The nervous system is charged with magnetic energy which fills us with peace and serenity. This state of mind enables us to gain a more balanced perspective on our actions and behaviour, showing us where we can make improvements. The alternate holding of hands in positions of giving and receiving establishes an exchange of energy between the partners.

24. HOW HAPPY WE ARE

Melody 24 – 32 bars

Description

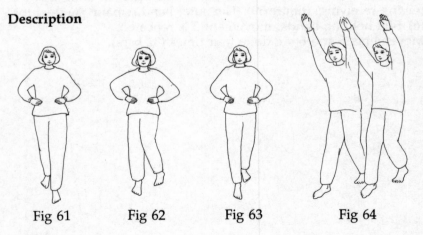

Fig 61   Fig 62   Fig 63   Fig 64

Starting position
Hands on hips, feet together.

Movements

First sequence
(1) Right foot steps forward with a slight joyous spring.
(2) Left foot steps forward likewise (figure 61).
(3) Right foot steps forward again, and left foot is lifted in the air on the toe (figure 62).
(4) The weight of the body is transferred back onto the left foot as it steps back on the spot; simultaneously the right leg is lifted in the air (figure 63).
Movements 1 to 4 are repeated.

Second sequence
(1) After the couple have grasped each other's inside hands, with the weight still on the left foot, the right foot steps forward with the left in the air; at the same time, the inside hands move forward and up in a circular motion, with the free hands mimicking the motion, palms forward (figure 64).
(2) The left foot steps forward and the right is lifted in the air; simultaneously the hands give a push forward and up.
(3) The body weight falls back onto the right foot, while the left is lifted in the air, bent at the knee; at the same time the hands swing down and back.
The above three movements are then repeated for 32 bars in all, but with feet reversed.

Hands are replaced on hips, and the whole sequence of movements is repeated.

Explanation

The music here moves up in the major key, expressing joy and elation, as well as gratitude for the gifts of life and nature. The second part helps us become aware of the forces of Living Nature: 'Life is a sacred gift – use this gift and work unceasingly with it, learning all the time. Whatever your circumstances, never lose your serenity'.

The rhythm and beat is an unusual one – 7/8 – originating from the Bulgarian folk dance known as '*rachenitsa*'. It is a most joyful dance requiring great mastery, agility and endurance.

If people express gratitude from morning to night for everything that surrounds them, the pure currents of Love will flow through their souls. Do not forget that all contradictions will eventually be resolved in the Great Divine Plan.

Whatever happens, everything will be changed for the better by the Universal Creative Forces which generate human development. Even in the direst of life's trials, the enlightened person is filled with joy.

25. STEP BY STEP

Melody 25 – 96 bars

Description

Fig 65

Fig 66

Starting position
Hands on hips, feet together.

Movements
(1) The right foot steps to the side on the toe (figure 65).
(2) The right foot returns to its starting position.
Repeat movements 1 and 2.
(3) The right foot steps forward on the toe (figure 66).
(4) The right foot once again returns to its starting position.
Repeat movements 3 and 4.
(5) The right foot steps forward, then the left, then the right again, before the left foot finally steps alongside the right.
The above movements 1 to 5 are repeated by the left foot, then again by the right foot and so on until the end of the music.

Explanation

The exercise develops patience and the insight that actions have to be prepared and then executed one step at a time. More specifically, when our legs are apart, we act as receivers of solar energy to the earth; and when our feet are together, we receive the earth's energy and transmit it towards the sun. Thus the dancers can gradually become aware of and distinguish solar and earth energy.

26. EARLY IN THE MORNING

Melody 26 – 96 bars

Description

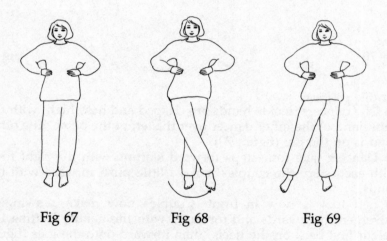

Fig 67   Fig 68   Fig 69

Starting position
Hands on hips with thumbs behind (figure 67).

Movements
First sequence
(1) The right foot describes a semi-circle in front of the left and points on the toe diagonally in front and to the left (figure 68).
(2) The right foot moves back out to the side and points out horizontally (figure 69).

(3) Identical to (1).

(4) The right foot swings back round and resumes its starting position next to the left.

(5) Take four steps forward, beginning with the right foot; on the fourth step, the left foot steps next to the right.

(6) Movements 1 to 5 are repeated inversely for the left foot.

These alternating movements continue until the end of the melody (24 bars).

Second sequence

Fig 70   Fig 71

Starting position

(7) The dancers' inside hands are clasped and held high, with the right hand of the inner dancer over the left of the outer. The other hand is on the hip (figure 70).

(8) Dancers take four steps forward starting with the right foot. With each step, the couples make a little push forward with the hands.

(9) Left foot is now in front. Couples now make a swinging movement backwards and forwards with the hands, shifting the weight first back on the heels, then forward onto the toes (figure 71). This is repeated, before a further four steps are taken and the sequence begins again.

Continue these movements until the end of the melody (24 bars).

Third sequence

(10) Hands on hips. The dancers then take four steps forward, starting on the right foot; on the fourth step, the left foot steps next to the right. The hands are flung forward, palms down, on steps 1 and 3, then back to hips on steps 2 and 4.

Fig 72   Fig 73

(11) The right foot then steps to the side, while the hands spread simultaneously out horizontally, palms down (figure 72).

(12) The right foot returns to its starting position, and the hands to the hips.

(13) Repeat movements 11 and 12.

(14) The right foot steps forward and arms stretch out parallel to the front, palms down (figure 73).

(15) Right foot steps back in place and hands return to hips.

(16) Repeat movements 14 and 15.

(17) Repeat movement 10.

The above sequence is repeated, this time starting with the left foot. The movements alternate until the end of the melody, which is played twice.

Explanation

The first sequence of this exercise, with its curved semi-circular movements of the feet, indicates the method of impregnating oneself with the energy of the earth. This energy is at its most powerful in the early morning and helps to harmonise the whole organism.

The second sequence, with partners holding each other by the hand and balancing backwards and forwards, is aimed at bringing into equilibrium our physical and mental capacities: the physical is represented by the heel, and the intellectual by the toes. We receive the corresponding energy through our feet.

The third sequence, using both arms and feet, expresses the strength of our resolve to accomplish our earthly task: 'The doors of the school of life are wide open for the person who loves their neighbour and dedicates their life to service of the Divine'.

27. Breathing

Description

Fig 74   Fig 75

Starting position
Dancers all face the centre, feet together, hands held in front the chest with palms facing inward and middle fingers nearly touching (figure 74).

Movements
(1) During the playing of the first long note the dancers inhale, simultaneously spreading their arms horizontally outwards until palms face the front (figure 75).
(2) While exhaling they sing the ascending scale on the vowel 'A', gradually bringing their hands back to the starting position.
These movements are repeated three times for each of the scales: the first ascending, the second descending, and the third both ascending and descending.

Explanation

The ascending scale symbolises human spiritual aspiration, the call to harmony. The descending scale symbolises the capacity to receive. The third mixed scale balances and harmonises the ascending and descending elements. The underlying meaning is to learn how to relate harmoniously and musically to each other and Nature.

The scale begins with 'A', the number 1, the number of the sun, the number of God, and unfolds all the colours of the rainbow corresponding to the individual notes.

Breathing develops the voice, while singing improves breathing.
Inhalation (inspiration) is synonymous with the soul.
Expiration is synonymous with the Spirit.
These are the two processes of Divine Love and Wisdom.

28. PROVIDENCE – BLESSING

Description

Fig 76

Starting position
Hands by the sides, dancers facing the centre.

Movements
(1) Arms are raised out to the side and over the head until the fingers are touching (figure 76). As one does this the first part of the formula is pronounced: 'May the Peace of God abide.'
(2) With fingers still touching, the hands are brought down to touch lightly the crown chakra on the top of the head. They then separate and travel down the side until the starting position is reached. The second part of the formula is pronounced: 'And may His pure Joy and sacred Exaltation arise in our hearts'.
The movements and formula are performed three times in all.

Explanation

The general movement is one of invoking a blessing as if one were pouring water over oneself. It means that we should freely accept the blessings of God in all their abundance. As the hands move up to join above the head, we enter into contact with the energy of the Divine World, which we bring into the physical world. The oneness and harmony of the Divine World is symbolised by the joining of the hands. They separate on entering the duality and polarity of the physical world at the crown chakra. The bringing down of the hands symbolises the transmission of the Divine Energy into the physical world: 'When people are in the physical world, they are at a distance from that reality which underlies creation. This exercise is a means of contacting the world of Divine ideas'.

CHAPTER FIVE

The Sunbeams

In most of the exercises in the first part of the paneurhythmy we have been on the outside wheel or circle of life, only approaching the centre on a few occasions. In this dance we enter the inside of the circle, acting as radii and facing towards the Centre of Divine Life – our source and destiny. Many movements in this sequence express the twin processes of evolution towards the Centre, where we gain inspiration and energy, followed by a movement out towards the periphery where we express and manifest what we have received.

This process is reflected by analogy on all planes of life. There are, for instance, two blood circulation currents in the human body – the arterial and the venous. The first moves from the centre to the periphery with purified blood, while the second returns from the periphery to the centre with venous blood in need of purification. The two processes are going on simultaneously.

A further parallel can be drawn with the circulation of electromagnetic currents between the sun and the earth. The current coming from the sun is arterial, while the reverse is venous, returning the sun's electromagnetic energy to be re-aligned with its rhythm. The movement of the twelve rays therefore expresses this great universal cosmic process, the rhythm of life itself.

In the 'Sunbeams' we are expressing the arrival of a Cosmic Spring, the advent of Love as a new power in the world. It will be clearer to explain the exact significance of the various movements as we proceed with the description, rather than insert it at the beginning or end.

INITIAL POSITION

The dancers are lined up in pairs forming, ideally, twelve rays facing the centre. There are six pairs in each radius sunray, making a total of 144 dancers. In the unlikely event of there being even more dancers, a circle of pairs is formed around the rays (figure 77). In practice, though, it is unlikely that there will be more than 30 dancers, which means that they form up in as many rays of six pairs as convenient.

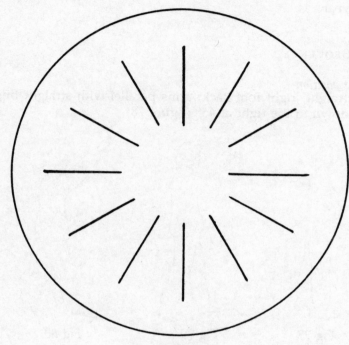

Fig 77

The distance between each partner and pair is about one metre, while the outer circle should be several metres away from the rays. The couples in the rays face the centre, while those on the outside have their left shoulders facing the centre.

The rays advance and retreat from the centre, while those on the outer circle move around the circumference. The pairs in the rays are arranged according to height, with the shorter at the front and the taller at the back.

Dancers may optionally join in with singing in the first six sequences, but all should sing during the seventh.

The twelve rays are the twelve gates of life referred to in Revelation 21 when St. John the Divine has the vision of a new heaven and a new earth. At the twelve gates are twelve angels, and

on the gates are inscribed the names of the twelve tribes of Israel.
The walls have twelve foundations, with the names of the twelve
apostles. The twelve gates are twelve pearls. The wall measures 144
cubits, or 12 times 12, the ideal number of dancers in 'Sunbeams'.
There are also twelve signs of the zodiac within the twelve months
of the year.

First Sequence

Starting position
Body straight, right foot back, arms parallel with straight fingers
facing down to the right at 45° (figure 78).

Fig 78   Fig 79   Fig 80

Figure 1. Advancing

Music: Theme 1 is played once.
(1) First two bars: step forward on the right foot, with the left foot
on the toe, parallel arms and hands swinging up at an angle of 45°
to the left with a light clap (figure 79).
(2) Bar 3: the body swings backwards with the weight falling on
the left foot. The right foot is raised with the knee slightly bent,
toes pointing down. Parallel hands swing gracefully down to the
left at an angle of 45°.
(3) Bars 4 and 5: Hands are thrown forward. Just as they are
passing the chest, the left foot takes a step forward and the right
foot is raised instead; simultaneously, the hands move forward

and up to the right at an angle of 45°, with palms down (*that is*, no clapping) (figure 80).
(4) Bar 6: hands swing back down to the starting position.
These same movements are repeated until the end of the theme, so that the hands move up three times to the left with a clap and twice to the right without clapping. At the last bar of the theme, the right foot remains forward.

Figure 2. Returning

Music: Theme 1 is played once.

Fig 81

(1) The hands are lightly placed on the waist, remaining in this position throughout the theme. The right foot moves in a semi-circle and is placed behind the left (figure 81).
(2) The left foot now makes the same semi-circular movement and is placed behind the right foot.
These movements continue, corresponding to one bar, for 15 steps backward. The body springs lightly during each movement.

The movement towards the centre represents our feet treading the path of Virtue. The first step is taken with joy – expressed in the clapping of the hands – as we have the feeling that we are on the right path – the path towards God. The symbolism of the moving towards and away from the centre has already been explained.

More specifically, though, the first clap is of the right hand over the left side of the body, denoting a transfer of the positive energy of the right hand to the negative or receptive left hand. The energy of the hands is harmonised, so that we can take a step forward with the hands moving in a flying motion up to the right. The balancing of our energies enables us to take a step forward. On the return, we pass what we have acquired in the centre to the periphery. The second advance in sequence 2 expresses the magnetic energy of the heart, while the third advance represents the balancing of the electromagnetic energies in the straight line of the will.

SECOND SEQUENCE

Starting position
The hands are still on the waist. The weight of the body is on the left foot.

Figure 1. Advancing

Music: Theme 2 is played once – 33 bars in all.

Fig 82

(1) The right foot which in the last figure remained behind moves with a semi-circular movement in front of the left foot a little to its left side and touches the ground with the toes, goes back with a semi-circular movement behind the left foot, all the time the weight of the body on the left foot. This movement of the right foot is repeated twice corresponding to the first four bars of the theme (figure 82).
(2) The right foot takes a step forward while the left foot is raised from the ground (bar 5). The left foot makes the same movements as described in (1) for five bars to the end of the theme.

The movement is repeated four times with the right foot and three times with the left. The last fourth movement of the right foot is incomplete: it makes a semi-circular movement forward, one backward, then another one forward, after which it returns to the beginning.

Figure 2. Returning

Music: Theme 3 is played once – 20 bars.
The return is as described in figure 2 of the first movement: 20 steps are taken backward. At the last bar the left foot remains behind.

THIRD SEQUENCE

Starting position
The hands are still on the waist. Weight of body is on the left foot.

Figure 1. Advancing

Music: Theme 4 is played twice with all the repetitions.

Fig 83

(1) Bars 1 – 3; The right foot with knee bent at a right angle is brought forward while the left foot lightly springs. The right foot touches the ground twice with the toes, the third time stepping forward receiving the weight of the body (figure 83).
(2) The left foot makes the same movements again for three bars. This is repeated six times with the right and six times with the left

foot. At the last bar the left foot is behind, but with a quick semi-circular movement forward it is prepared for the return.

Figure 2. Returning

Music: Theme 5 is played once.
Returning is the same way, as described in number 2 of the first movement. Thirteen steps are taken backward then the right foot is placed by the left and one is ready for the next figure.

FOURTH SEQUENCE

Starting position
Body straight, hands on waist, feet together.

Figure 1. Single circling

Music: The first part of theme 6.

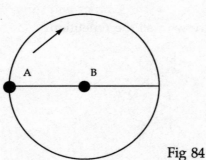 

Fig 84

(1) At the start of the music the left partner of every couple takes ten rhythmic lightly springing steps around his partner on the right. The steps are graceful with lightly bent knee. Step on the toes with a slight springing movement of the body. The circle is described in such a way that the left partner turns to the right, passing in front of his partner then turns and continues moving behind his partner back to his starting position (figure 84).
(2) During this time the right partner remains on the spot, the weight of his body on the left foot, while the right foot is brought forward and taps the ground four times with the toes and lightly

bent knee; at the fifth beat it steps back to its place. Then the left foot is brought forward and taps the ground four times and on the fifth beat steps back.

Figure 2. Performance on the spot

Music: The second part of theme 6 is played.

Fig 85

All tap the ground three times with the toes of the right foot lightly touching the ground. Then the right foot steps back on the fourth beat (figure 85). Then the left foot taps three times and steps back on fourth beat.

FIFTH SEQUENCE

Starting position
Body straight, feet together, hands on waist (figure 86).

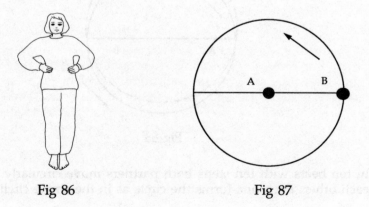

Fig 86   Fig 87

Figure 1. Single circling

Music: The first part of theme 6.
The right partner of every couple circles the left one as described in the last figure. He passes in front to the side and behind to the starting position. All this is done in ten steps. While moving he steps on his toes with a light springing movement of the body (figure 87).

During this time the left partner makes the same movements as described in the figure for the left partner.

Figure 2. Performance on the spot

Music: The second part of theme 6.
All do the same tapping as in number 2 of the fourth sequence.

SIXTH SEQUENCE

Starting position
Body straight. Hands on waist. Feet together.

Figure 1. Double circling

Music: The first part of theme 6.

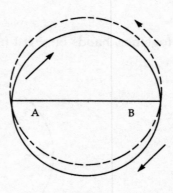

Fig 88

In ten beats with ten steps both partners move circularly around each other. Each one forms the circle as in the single circling, but when they are moving in the front part of the circle, the right partner describes the external semi-circle, while at the back – the left partner describes the semi-circle (external) (figure 88).

Figure 2. Performance on the spot

Music: The second part of theme 6.
All do the same rhythmic taps as in the second figure of the fourth sequence.
After finishing the circling, sequences 4, 5 and 6 are repeated once more.
Sequences 4 to 6, the circling movements, express the historic phase of human development when we are enclosed in the limiting circle of matter. There has been a gradual sinking into matter, with a concomitant loss of spiritual awareness and values as we arrive at a materialistic culture and outlook. We lose our consciousness of the reality of the higher realms of the spirit, and even come to deny their very existence. In Indian terms, we are bound to the wheel of Samsara. The exit from the closed circle, represented in the movements which follow, marks the awakening of the soul from its slumbering state in matter.

SEVENTH SEQUENCE

Music: Theme 7.

Fig 89

The couples draw closer to each other taking hold of each other's hands. The inner hands are raised high above their heads, the outside hands are held a bit below the solar plexus so that the hands held together form a lovely wreath (figure 89). In this position all sing theme 7.

Eighth Sequence

Music: Theme 8.

Fig 90

At the start of the music containing thirteen bars, the hands lightly clap in front of the chest – the active right hand over the left. The hands clap at the beginning of each bar. After each clap the hands open up a little higher. This movement expresses the principle of liberation. At the same time all sing theme 8: Rai, rai rai . . . (figure 90).

Ninth Sequence

Music: The first part of theme 9.

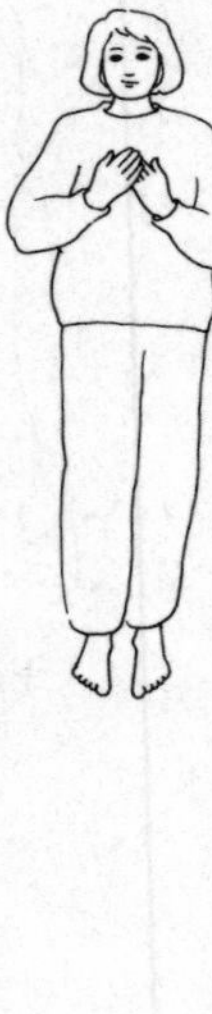

Fig 91 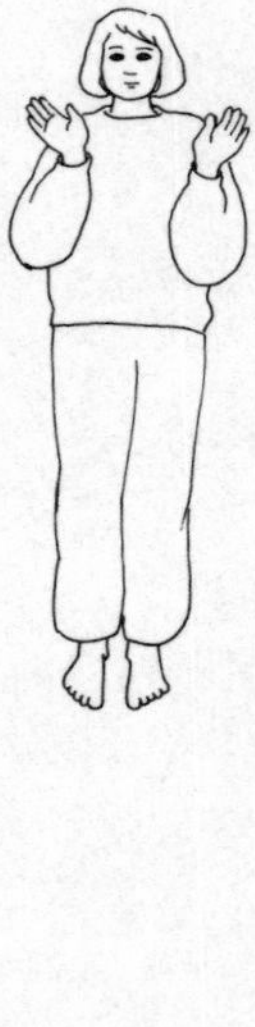   **Fig 92**

The words 'Kaji mi, kaji mi, kaji mi, sladki dumi dve' are sung twice (Tell me two sweet words!).

Figure 1

(1) Both hands bent at the elbows are placed on the chest, right hand over left with palms inwards. At the moment of the placing of the hands is sung the word 'kaji'. (figure 91).

(2) Then singing the word 'mi' the hands open to the sides in bow fashion like the opening of a flower, each hand describing a bow not more than 90°. This movement expresses blossoming (figure 92).

The same movements are repeated to the end of the theme, the hands interchanging positions – first the right hand is on top, then the left and again the right, etc. The hands are over one another every first two syllables/beats, opening on the third beat.

Figure 2

Music: The second part of theme 9.

All sing the words 'Tvoite dumi dve, sladki dumi dve' twice. The two hands are placed one on the other as described before, palms inwards, the right hand on the left. While in this position the words 'Tvoite dumi dve' are sung. Opening the hands, the words 'sladki dumi dve' are sung. All this is repeated twice. On the repetition the left hand is over the right one.

TENTH SEQUENCE

Music: Theme 10.

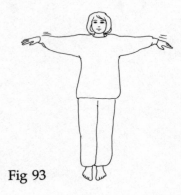

Fig 93

All sing the words 'Tui e rai' (This is paradise) three times and the words 'Tui e rai, rai', while the arms are stretched horizontally at the level of the shoulders making five light wavelike movements resembling flying. End with a little shaking of the wrists. The song and the five movements are repeated once more (figure 93).

The abstract description of these exercises does not convey to one a sufficient idea of the movements, since they are unceasing and flowing. That is why it is desirable that the dancer should first see them and try them out. This text will serve then as a reminder.

The awakening of the soul is the dawn of freedom and light, the liberation from slavery and darkness into a world of joy. The words sung express the sentiment: 'You have given birth to me, Mother (earth), a beautiful person, so as to become clever, to think well and to love well; this is the Life of Paradise'. The Life of Love and Wisdom is the Life of Paradise. The emergence of the soul is like the germinated grain of wheat which pierces the ground and reaches towards the light for the first time.

The eighth sequence expresses the joy felt after entering into this new world. The hands clap together, active right on top, and gradually ascend to symbolise the upward elan to the soul.

In the ninth sequence, the placing of the hands over each other harmonises the two currents of hot and cold, magnetic and electric, heart and mind. The opening out signifies the blossoming which can take place as a result of the harmonisation.

In the tenth sequence, accompanied by feelings of exquisite spiritual nostalgia expressed by the wistful music, the arms stretch out to the side in a flying motion. The soul is free from all limitations, the fruit is ripe; we find ourselves once more in our native element, we have reached home again.

CHAPTER SIX

The Pentagram

The Pentagram is the symbol of the Cosmic Man. It is performed in a circle, which symbolises the development of the Cosmic Man on his endless path of development.

THE WORDS OF THE PENTAGRAM

> Here we come
> Luminous rays,
> Bearing a royal and blessed gift:
> Joy, peace and love,
> Light and living beauty,
> And freedom to all noetic beings.
> We are the rays of the sun of love,
> We have come to earth to conquer evil
> So as to establish peace.
> With blessing, light and gentle love,
> We will establish a new life
> Throughout the world.

THE MEANING OF THE PENTAGRAM

As indicated above, the Pentagram represents the Cosmic Man. It is also the Way of the Disciple, the path which must be trodden for the attainment of perfection. The head symbolises Truth, the right leg Equity, the right arm Wisdom, the left leg Virtue, and the left arm Love. To the basis of Beinsa Douno's teaching on the principles of Love, Wisdom and Truth are added the 'legs' of Equity and Virtue. These five essential or principal qualities need to

be attained on the path to perfection. The Master received the explanation of the Pentagram in 1898, but only gave it out to his disciples at the annual Congress in Ternovo in August of 1914. The symbol was used in the ancient Pythagorean initiatic schools but its meaning has hitherto never been so fully elucidated.

The tip of the Pentagram – Truth – is light blue, the colour of the spiritual person. The tip of Love is pink, the colour of the heart and lungs. The tip of Wisdom is light yellow, the colour of the intellect. The tip of Equity is orange the colour of bile and the liver. Finally, the tip of Virtue is green, the colour of the grass.

If the meaning of the principles of Love, Wisdom and Truth is easily comprehensible, that of equity, or Justice, has a much deeper sense than is ordinarily understood. The equitable human being is one who respects all living creatures because of the knowledge that God is present in all created forms. All have their place in the Divine Economy. By mistreating an animal, for instance, one infringes the law of Equity. The goods dispensed by God should be equitably shared out between all beings; all should benefit from them.

What is meant by the notion of Virtue in this context? Love, Wisdom, Truth and Equity are all virtues. In its broadest sense, it includes all virtues, while in a narrower sense it means the accomplishment of good actions; in an even more specific sense it represents the service of God: the person who serves God is virtuous.

Outside the Pentagram are the three letters V, U, J, or Velikito Uchilishde na Jivota (Great School of Life). The Pentagram illustrates the way in which Life represents a school of experience. Every experience teaches us something, everything we meet on our way helps us to advance and develop our talents and virtues. We learn not only from communicating with human beings, but also with other forms of creation like flowers and trees. We also see the numbers 1–5, designating the five virtues.

The Pentagram consists of three parts: an outer circle, an inner part, and the centre. The surrounding circle represents the world of experience on earth; in itself, the circle symbolises the infinite – the possibility of acquiring in the course of eternity what is impossible over a short lifetime. We shall explain the significance of each of the phases of the pentagram in their order of development. In practice, it may seem that we find ourselves at various stages at once, but the overall direction is clear.

THE OUTER PART OF THE PENTAGRAM

First Picture – The Sword

The soul is here at the beginning of its development. The sword denotes the way of violence and injustice, pursued in ignorance of the karmic consequences ensuing from such actions.

Second Picture – The Cup

The bitter cup is that of suffering, the inevitable outcome of the violence which engenders further violence. Suffering in this sense is a method for awakening the human soul to the realisation that violence and injustice are not the right procedure: the suffering is meant to teach this lesson. This connection may not be fully realised at the time, but Beinsa Douno explains that the soul will clearly perceive this connection on entering the invisible world after death, resolving to avoid such methods in future incarnations.

Two other meanings of suffering are mentioned in relation to this image: firstly, that suffering transmutes to Love, that the present sufferings of humanity are preparing the person of Love. Beinsa Douno compares this process with the churning of milk to make butter. Milk symbolises Love, and the churning of suffering is a temporary phenomenon which will disappear from life when its causes are removed.

The final meaning is suffering as a means of refining the organism in order to receive and contain the seed ideas of the new culture. This kind of suffering corresponds to birth pangs. We are assured that the gradual refinement of the human organism will eliminate the need for this suffering before the reception of new ideas.

Third Picture – The Book

The book follows the cup, as people begin to study the Book of Life and learn the laws governing life as a result of the suffering incurred. This is the beginning of the acquisition of spiritual knowledge.

Fourth Picture – The Candle

When a person reads the Book of Life and begins to understand the processes of nature, they gain some illumination – a new light, symbolised by the candle, illumines our consciousness. This candle or light enables us to appreciate the majesty and beauty of the Divine Plan which leads us from darkness to Light, from slavery to Freedom, from imperfection to Perfection, from sinfulness to Purity and from ignorance to Knowledge.

Fifth Picture – The Sceptre

The reading of the book and the influx of illumination gradually enable us to gain control over ourselves and attain self-mastery, symbolised by the sceptre – the emblem of power. We can freely abstain from expressing our lower nature, having learned to control it. The sceptre also represents the stage of beginning to use certain natural powers and laws under the aegis of the law of Equity.

This completes the outer circle of human development, representing the life and path of the worldly person. This whole stage is traversed unconsciously, and brings the person to an inner crisis or turning point characterised by a vague sense of unease and dissatisfaction which encourages them to seek a deeper meaning in life. The entering into the Pentagram is the commitment on the path of the disciple.

THE INNER PART OF THE PENTAGRAM

The outer Pentagram path may take hundreds of years and countless incarnations to complete. By this stage, the person has already been consciously doing inner work towards refinement and perfection in a process of taking charge of their own spiritual development. Here too are five pictures, which we shall explain in order.

First Picture – Staircase Leading to a Door

Entering upon the Way of the Disciple marks the beginning of spiritual trials which are easier in the first phase. The convenient steps symbolise the relatively less arduous initial trials or tests. Three examples are given: if in a trying situation you lose your courage or inner peace, you have failed the test; if you lost something valuable and still retain your self-possession and presence of mind, you have passed the test; if you pass a suffering human being and receive the impulse to help, but disregard it, you have failed the test.

This stage of the disciple's development is the dawning of Truth, the birth of an awareness of God, who is Truth. The disciple receives an impulse to walk in the Path of God and to accomplish His Will. This Truth will only shine in its pristine fullness when the disciple has attained perfection.

Second Picture – Christ

At the summit of the Pentagram is the figure of Christ, with whom the disciple begins to form a bond. Christ is the manifestation of God: His Spirit begins to work within the disciple with inner promptings so that a change is brought about as we begin to enter the path of Equity and Justice: respecting all living creatures for the

Divine, which lives within them and the right they all have to favourable conditions of development.

Third Picture – The Steep, Stony Path and Narrow Door

This is the narrow gate spoken of by Christ and which requires a certain renunciation of the things of this world. The disciple will seek to help and succour the afflicted, and to accomplish the good actions inwardly suggested. The climbing of the steep and stony path leading to the narrow door is achieved at the expense of the personality, impelled as the disciple is to work in serving God.

One of the tests of this phase is to love and forgive our enemies. Real forgiveness is accompanied by love. Another test is a variant of the trial of Job, the passing through a great illness or loss which may tempt us to lose our faith and the sense that all such events are ultimately for a good end. Such a hard trial is an initiatory test. Another test would be for the disciple to deny the connection with God for the sake of wealth, glory or power. Having passed through these kinds of test, the disciple is ready to receive Love and enter the true Life. It is as if life hitherto has been a preparation for this moment.

Fourth Picture – The Eye

The eye symbolises light and wisdom: 'the light of the body is the eye: if therefore thine eye be single, thy whole body shall be full of light' (Matthew 6:22). The disciple has a deeper understanding of things, having received Divine Wisdom. In the outer circle we acquired outer knowledge but we now enter the realm of Divine Wisdom. The door of the Temple of Wisdom opens up, but only for the person of Love. Only such a person can safely be entrusted with the keys to Higher Knowledge and not make use of it for personal ends. This Knowledge should only be used in the service of God and all beings. A person entrusted with such Knowledge before passing through Love will simply misuse it, bringing great misfortune on themselves and others around them.

Fifth Picture – The Tree of Life

After having acquired Love, Wisdom, Truth and Equity, the disciple comes to the Tree of Life. This new conception of life begins to bear fruit as we enter into the path of Virtue, that of benevolence and accomplishment of good actions. Real good springs from Love, and its highest expression is in the service of God. The idea dawns that the only meaning in life consists in serving God. The Master Beinsa Douno states that 'to manifest Love is to serve God'. The highest form of such service is to show others the way to God, to work for the awakening of their consciousness so that they can come to know God and start working in this way themselves.

This picture marks the end of the path of the inner Pentagram, the acquisition of the cardinal virtues. The path towards the summit of Truth, the Path of the Master, is vertical. We enter the centre of the Pentagram, meditating on the profound inner meaning of life and Divine Laws.

THE CENTRE OF THE PENTAGRAM

The third and final phase of development is represented by the centre of the Pentagram, where we find two intertwined snakes, then a circle with a cross and another circle on top. The two snakes symbolise the struggle with our lower nature which must be conquered by passing through the cross – complete renunciation – with a view to directing our efforts to the single goal of serving God.

This is the way leading to perfection, to eternal life, to immortality; it is a way of absolute self-denial and supreme devotion to the Divine Cause in serving God and humanity. We rise to a higher manifestation of Love through sacrifice, passing through the most terrible tests: total self-renunciation is the price of integral union with God.

Before we enter the Divine Centre, there is one ultimate test, the test of Golgotha, the greatest sufferings during which the disciple will feel alone and abandoned, overwhelmed by a great gloom in the dark night of the soul. Although we think ourselves bereft, we are actually sustained and watched over by beings of light who are wishing that we should not fail this most arduous of all tests. At such a moment we need to remember that there is One who loves us and is always with us – God. God is our only support at such a dark hour. If we achieve this consciousness, we enter into the new life of resurrection, the life of blessedness, joy, light and freedom. Our mind and heart are developed, our will tempered, our being purified by the scourge of initiatory sufferings.

After having realised the Pentagram within ourselves, that is when the five great Principles are operating in and through us, we are united with the Divine World and have become a conscious noetic entity who knows how to work for human evolution in the light of a knowledge of Divine Laws acquired through the appropriation of Divine Wisdom.

The crown of our achievements is to realise the profound truth of the formula 'In the fulfilment of the Will of God lies the power of the human soul'. It should be pronounced with great concentration. As mentioned above, these words are inscribed around the outer circle. Outside and around the outer circle, it is written: 'God so loved the world that he sent his only-begotten Son so that whoever believes on Him should not perish but gain eternal Life'. Finally, on the very outside, one reads: 'Seek ye first the Kingdom of God, and all else shall be added unto you'. Although these texts for the outer circles are not actually written down, they represent a powerful combination when used together in prayer.

The first formula can be expanded as follows:

> In the fulfilment of the will of God by means of Love lies the power of the human soul.
> In the fulfilment of the will of God by means of Wisdom lies the power of the human soul.
> In the fulfilment of the will of God by means of Truth lies the power of the human soul.
> In the fulfilment of the will of God by means of Equity lies the power of the human soul.
> In the fulfilment of the will of God by means of Virtue lies the power of the human soul.

According to the quality with which you wish to work, you set it up with the tip pointing upwards.

In a conversation about the Pentagram, the Master once said 'Some people consider the Pentagram a lifeless and ineffectual form, but they are deceiving themselves. The Pentagram is a source of life and light. The Pentagram constantly emits light which is spread around like rays. Why? Because it is not an ordinary shape, but is constructed on the basis of occult spiritual laws. Such forces act within it'.

The Pentagram should always be placed with a single point upwards, never with a single point downwards or inverted, in which case its effects can be negative. It emits light in all directions with its strong emanations. If worn, we should be aware of its symbolic power. It also constitutes a protective zone and can be used to place ourselves under protection. It can be drawn and visualised around the body, for instance just before going to sleep. It should be drawn starting from the right foot, going up to the head, down to the left foot, across to the right arm, then the left arm, before coming back down to the right foot.

The Pentagram has a powerful protective role, and so the person wearing it should also try to maintain their purity and integrity, lest the symbol amplify some negative thoughts and feelings, turning them back against ourselves. We should have the firm resolve to serve God at all times and in all places. In this way, the immense spiritual and mystical power of the Pentagram will be used to best effect as we proceed on our path of unfolding and development.

INSTRUCTIONS FOR THE PERFORMANCE OF THE PENTAGRAM

The players are arranged in straight radial rows (figure 95). Each row consists of five pairs. The central pair symbolises the head of Cosmic Man. On the two sides of the head are the feet and the two pairs at the ends symbolise the hands. Ideally, there should be twelve radial rows with ten people in each row but if the number is smaller, the Pentagram can consist of fewer rows.

With the starting of the music given by the Master Beinsa Douno, all rows walk forward perpendicularly to the radius of the circle as shown in figure 96. The whole row takes eight steps forward (or 4 bars); at each step with the right foot the hands are thrown open to the sides forming a straight line. At each step with the left foot the arms bend at the elbows horizontally and the hands are placed on the chest with the palms turned down. The 'feet' stop after eight steps, but the 'head' and 'hands' keep going. After eight more steps the 'hands' stop, while the 'head' takes eight more steps (figure 97). Four bars follow during which all pairs turn facing the centre (figure 98). During this turning, each pair makes a small adjustment so that the regular figure of the Pentagram may be formed.

Up to this moment the music has played 16 bars, after which the movement of the pairs begins in the following way (figure 99a). The head moves to the place of the right foot, the right foot becomes left hand, the left hand becomes right hand, the right hand becomes left foot, and the left foot becomes head. The exchanging of these places is performed in two stages. First the inside players start moving (figure 99b). When they come to their assigned place, the second dancer takes a step forward to make room for the approaching dancer.

This movement is repeated as the second members of each pair move to the place behind their partners (figure 99c and d). In practice this means moving towards the pair second on the left.

When all this is accomplished the coming together of the pairs in each row begins (figure 100). The left hand and the head remain in their place, while the left and right foot start moving. When the right foot falls in line with the right hand, the latter pair also starts forward until the pairs reach their assigned places shown in figure 101. The right foot takes the place between the head and the right hand, but the left foot is placed between the left hand and the head. Thus the whole row lines up radially (figure 102). After that, all the rows move forward fan-like (figure 103), each row carefully keeping a radial position to the centre. This requires the left end of each row to take smaller steps so that the right end should not be forced to run. This way every row takes 32 steps (for 16 bars).

From figure 95 to figure 102 the hands move continuously in the way described above (see figures 104 and 105). But in figure 103 the arms make circular movements with the hands being thrown up forcefully and coming down to the sides of the body, as shown in figures 106 and 107.

This cycle from figures 95–103 is repeated the same way five times after which each pair has been head, left and right foot and left and right hand. This means that every human soul undergoes the experiences of the five basic principles with which the Cosmic Man is linked: Love, Wisdom, Truth, Equity and Virtue. In this way, the human soul acquires the experiences necessary to complete development. When all the rows have performed the five cycles here described, the partners of each pair shake hands cordially, because by means of the Pentagram they are already linked in the heart of the Great Cosmic Man.

EXPLANATION OF THE FIGURES OF THE PENTAGRAM

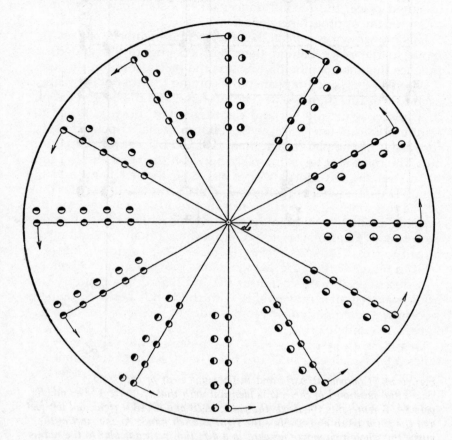

Figure 95. *A general plan of the starting position.*
The players are lined in radial rows in a circle with the centre. The ideal
number of rows is twelve but in practice there may be fewer rows. Each row
consists of five pairs. The players are marked by ◐ , ◖ *is the front and* ◗ *the*
back side of the player.

The arrows show the direction of the movement of the rows. The players are
lined one behind the other facing the direction of the movement. Hands down
at the sides.

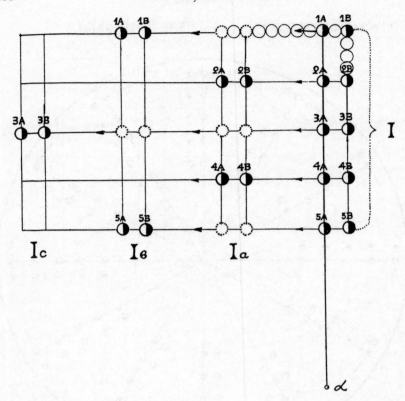

Figure 96. *Component parts and initial movement of each row.*
The initial position I of the row is identical with that of figure 1. The middle
pair 3A3B represents the head, the pairs 2A2B and 4A4B – right and left foot
and the pairs 1A1B and 5A5B – the right and left hand. At the start of the
music the whole row moves forward in a direction perpendicular to the radius
of the circle with the centre ∝. The steps start with the right foot, while at
the same time the arms open horizontally sideways, forming a straight line.
The second step with the left foot, the arms bend at the elbows horizontally
and the hands are placed on the chest with the palms turned down (see figure
104 and 105). After the whole row has taken eight steps forward, for four
bars, the feet 2A2B and 4A4B stop in place (position 1a). The rest of the pairs
continue taking eight more steps after which the hands 1A1B and 5A5B stop
moving in the position 1b. The head 3A3B takes eight more steps forward to
the position 1c.
   The empty circles ○ represent the interspace positions of the player marked
by ◑. The empty circles ○ between 1B and 2B show the real distance between
two pairs in the row. The dotted circles ○ show the place of the player in his
previous positions. The arrows show the direction of the movement.

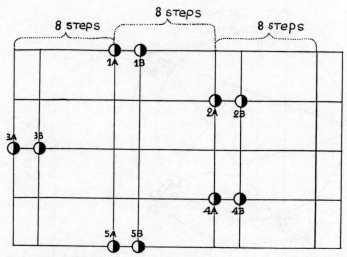

Figure 97. *Final position of the players after the rectilinear movement of the rows described in figure 96.*

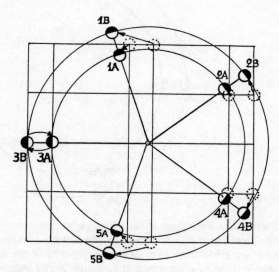

Figure 98. *Initial position for forming the Pentagram.*
From the initial position marked by dotted circles (same as figure 97), the players move for four bars as shown by the arrows in the figure to their new position in which every pair takes a place at the end of each ray of the Pentagram, facing the centre. The arms continue with the movements to the sides and in front of the chest as described in figure 104 and 105.

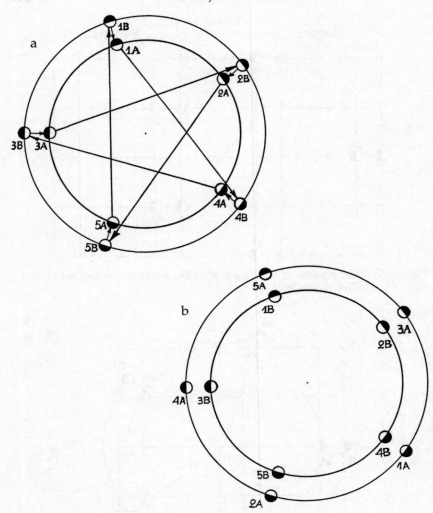

Figure 99a and 99b. *The unfolding of the Pentagram.*
(A) From the initial position shown in figure 98 the players 1A, 2A, 3A, 4A, 5A, occupying the inner circle move simultaneously forward in the direction marked for each one of them by a big arrow (i.e. behind to the left). 1A moves towards 4B, 2A towards 5B, 4A towards 3B, 5A towards 1A and 3A towards 2B. When 1A, 2A, 3A, 4A and 5A approach their corresponding partners, 4B, 5B, 2B, 3B and 1B take a step forward marked by a small arrow and then 1A, 2A, 3A, 4A and 5A take their place behind their partners. The movement of the hands is the same as in figure 96.
(B) Final position of the players after the movements described in (A).

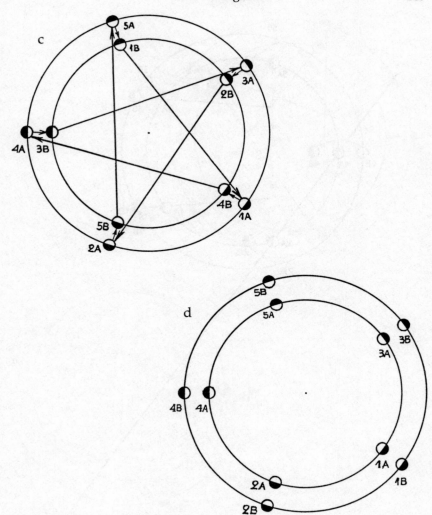

(C) *The movements of the players described in A are repeated the same way. The players of the inner circle 1B, 2B, 3B, 4B and 5B move and take their place correspondingly behind 1A, 2A, 3A, 4A, and 5A.*
(D) *Final position of the players after the movements described in (C) in which the initial pairs stand together again.*

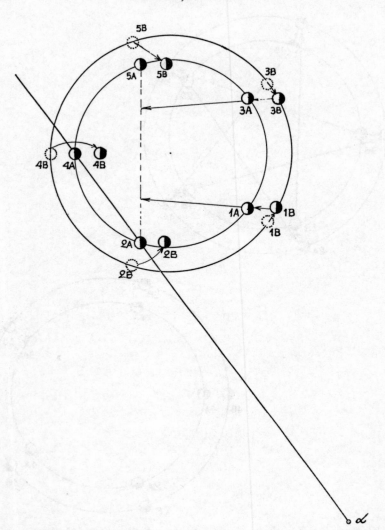

Figure 100. *Folding the Pentagram.*
The players 1B, 2B, 3B, 4B and 5B move as shown by the arrows in the figure
and take their place behind their corresponding partners. The pairs 4A4B,
5A5B and 2A2B turn face forward. The pairs 3A3B and 1A1B start forward as
shown by the arrow. The arms move as described in figure 10.

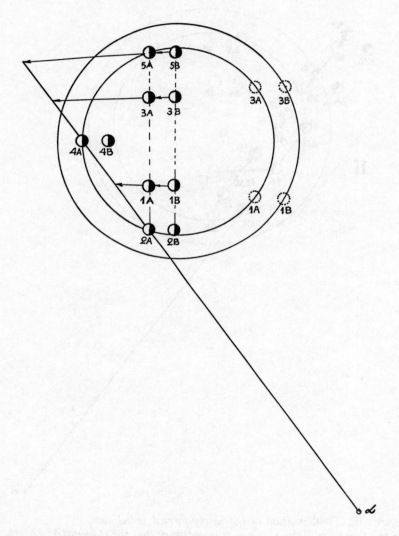

Figure 101. *Forming the radial row.*
The pairs 4A4B and 2A2B are placed as a radius of the circle with the centre α
and remain in their place. When the pair 3A3B falls in line with pair 5A5B, it
starts moving forward and all pairs continue moving forward until they reach
the places shown by arrows on the radius of the circle with the centre. The
arms move as in figure 10.

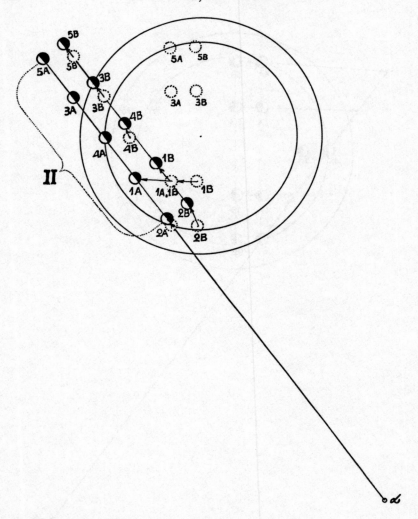

Figure 102. *Final position of the newly formed radial row.*
For the formation of the new row it is necessary that the players 1A, 2A, 1B,
2B, 3B, 4B and 5B should take an additional small step from the positions
marked by the dotted circles ○ *to the positions marked by the half-filled circles*
◐ *in the direction given by a corresponding arrow. The row from the position*
1/figure 96 has taken the position 2, as in the newly formed row the places of
the pairs are changed as follows: the head 3A3B has become right foot; the
right foot 2A2B has become left hand; the left hand 5A5B has become right
hand; the right hand 1A1B has become left foot and the left foot 4A4B has
become head.

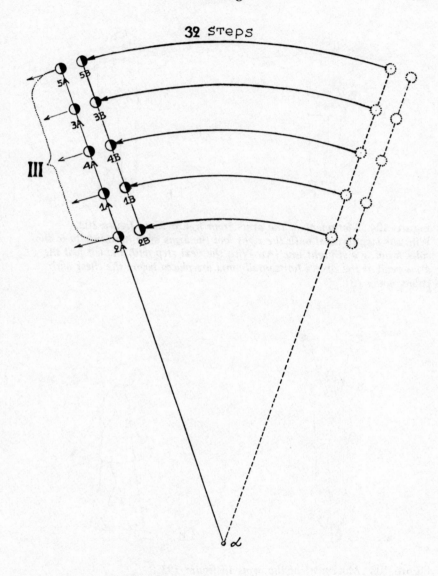

Figure 103. *Radial movement of the row.*
The whole row starts forward with the right foot. The hands are thrown up
forcefully with palms turned forward. With the step of the left foot the hands
come down to the sides of the body with a circular motion (see figures 106 and
107), 32 steps are taken which ends the first cycle. The new position 3 of the
row is ready for the next cycle.

Figure 104. *Movement of the arms from figure 95 to figure 102.*
With the step forward with the right foot the arms open horizontally to the
sides forming a straight line (A). With the next step with the left foot the
arms bend at the elbows horizontally and are placed before the chest with
palms down (B).

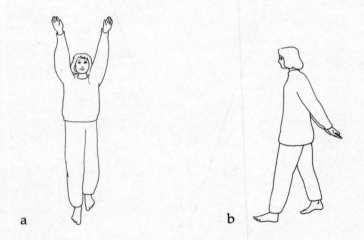

Figure 105. *Movement of the arms in figure 103.*
With the first step forward with the right foot the arms are thrown up
forcefully (A). At the next step with the left foot the arms return to the sides
in bow-like fashion (B). (i.e. describing a circle outwards).

CHAPTER SEVEN

Music and Translation of the Words

PHONETIC KEY

English approximation

U as in but
tz as in Ritz
ck as in check
ch as in loch

PANEURHYTHMY

1. AWAKENING

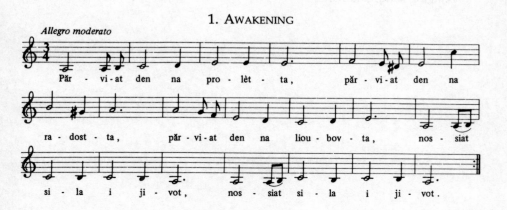

Here is the first day of spring,
The first day of joy,
The first day of love,
Bringing strength and life.

2. RECONCILIATION

I o-ji-via-va i ni bou-di săs liou-bov.

Sta - vaï - té ot săn, dè - ça! Pro - let mi - la věč doï - dé.

Çé - la - ta pri - ro - da pé - è. Slăn - çé top - lo vě - čě gréï.

Nos - si çvé - tia i plo - do - vé, nos - si pés - ni i i - gri.

It revives us and awakens us with love.
Arise from your sleep, children!
Sweet spring is here,
The whole of Nature sings.
A warm sun is already shining on everything,
Bringing flowers and fruit,
Bringing songs and dance.

3. GIVING

Păl - ni vsé - ka tvar s'ji - vot, bou - di ra - dost văv dou-
-hăt, raz - vès - sè - lia - va săr - ça - ta ni.
Gré - è, gréï, slăn - çé - to bla - go - dat - no,
çé - lou - va néj - no çé - la - ta zè - mia,
i ia ou - kič - va s'prè - lest - ni bèz - broï çvè - tia.

It fills every being with life,
Awakening joy in the spirit,
Gladdening every heart.
Shine! Shine! Bountiful sun
Tenderly embracing the whole earth,
Decorating her with a host of
delightful flowers.

4. ASCENDING

And the stars like diamonds shining
Are whispering ancient tales,
And the pure moon
Ceaselessly glides
On her cosmic path.
And a new day
Follows the night.

5. ELEVATION

The sun brings strength and joy,
Youth and love.
It inspires us and
Makes us grow in beauty.

6. OPENING 7. LIBERATION 8. CLAPPING

E - to go, raj - da cè kras - siv - i den.   E - to go,
Nié pla - ni - ni té o - bi - că - mè. Div - ni - ya

slăn - çé - to kăm na - zi gréï.   Him - ni v'go - ra - ta
Mous - sa - la văz - pé - va - mè. Pri sèd-mo - strou - na

vès - sè - lo pti - čen - çè peï.   Bo - dro i
ar - fa - na Ri - la sé - dim.   Mocht - no - to

gra - èm po ros - ni trè - vi i çvé - tia.
slăn - çè po - sré - chta-mè na ra - ni - na.

Své - tla - ta ra - dost o - bil - no ni gréï.
Vè - čer si - yaï - ni - tè zvèz - di slè - dim

Si - la v'dou - cha - ta bèz - spir - no iz - li - va - ni tia.
i lou - na - ta prè - krass - na v'nè - bess - na - ta chir.

OPENING

Here is the dawn of a beautiful day.
The sun is shining upon us,
The birds are merrily singing in the woods.
With sprightly step we dance
Through the dewy grass and flowers.
Radiant joy shines abundantly upon us,   )
Constantly pouring strength into our souls.) Repeat

LIBERATION

We are in love with the mountains.
We glorify the divine Moussala,
While sitting by the seven Rila Lakes.
At dawn we await the mighty sun.
In the evening twilight sky
We follow the beautiful moon and the shining stars.

CLAPPING

As for No. 7

9. PURIFICATION

Păr - vi - at den na pro - lét - ta, păr - vi - at den na
ra - dost - ta, păr - vi - at den na liou - bov - ta, nos - siat
si - la i ji - vot, nos - siat si - la i ji - vot.

Music and lyrics as for No. 1

10. FLYING

I zě - mia - ta sè să - bouj - da ot să - nia.

Poč - va no - vi své - tăl den, no - vi - ia den na

pro - lèt - ta. I pri - ro - da - ta li - kou - va,

čè ia slăn - cé top - lo grèï, i lă - či o -

bil - no lèï. Vsič - ko rad - va sé i pèï.

The Earth is awakening from its dream.
A bright new day begins,
A bright new day of spring.
The whole of nature celebrates,
In the warm sun shining upon it
With penetrating rays.
The whole creation rejoices and sings

11. EVERA

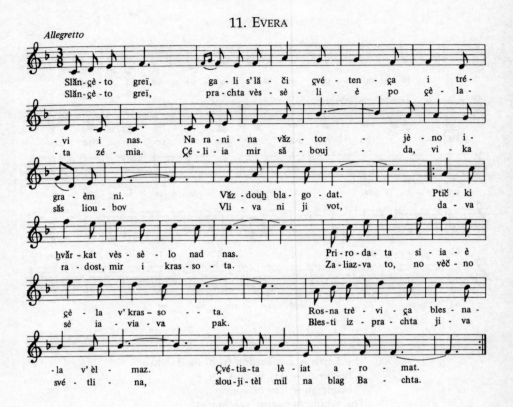

The shining sun gently strokes
The flowers, the grass and all of us.
At dawn we dance with delight
In the rich abundant air.
The birds flutter merrily above us,
The whole of Nature is radiant and shining with beauty,
The dewy grass gleams like a diamond,
The flowers exhale a heavenly scent.

The shining sun showers the entire world with gaiety,
Awakening the whole earth with a call of love.
It fills us with life,
Giving us joy, peace and beauty.
It sets and always rises again,
Shining and spreading living light,
A cherished servant of our tender Heavenly Father.

12. JUMPING

Na go-rè da po-lè-tim kăm nè-bes-ni-ia pro-stor. S'mir, liou-bov i své-tli-na na vsič-ko ra-sté v'kras-so-ta, i ni nos-si mă-dros-ta.

Let us all take off towards the heavenly realms,
With peace and love and light.
Everything grows into beauty
And brings us wisdom.

13. WEAVING

Every day, every hour, every minute
We are weaving the most beautiful thoughts.
May a pure and holy life
Flow into our souls.
May peace and love pervade our hearts.
May goodness and kindness live within us,
May light and gaiety shine everywhere.
The flowers gently fill the air with their sweet scent,
The birds in the celestial sky twitter and sing.
A gentle rain falls upon the fields and meadows.
So every day, every hour, every minute
We will work and grow, sowing goodness
And weaving beautiful thoughts in our souls.

14. Thinking

Think! Think rightly!
Think! Think rightly!
Support your life
With sacred thoughts!

15. Aoum

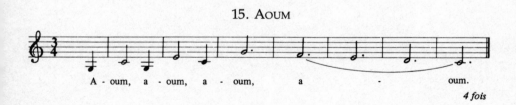

16. THE RISING SUN

The sun is rising,
Spreading its light
And bringing joy for life.
Living strength is
Springing from the source!
All of our life,
May it be so!

17. SQUARE

The sun is shining,
The dawn sparkles with life and love.
The dawn sparkles,
Shining with brilliant shafts of light.
Everything sings today,
Everything sweetly sings today,
Praising the Lord's new day,
Praising the Lord's new day,
For the new joy,
Which ceaselessly flows into our hearts.

18. FLEXIBILITY 19. BEAUTY

Vsé - ka   sou - trin   v'ra - nen   čas   slăn - çè - to   po - srè - chta - mé.

Lă - či,   văz - douh   i   ros - sa   rad - vat   na - chi - té   săr - ça.

Vdăh - no - vè - ni   mis - li   v'nas   da   po - tè - kat.
Slad - ki   zré - li   plo - do - vé   da   da - vat,

I   kras - si - vi   čouv - stva   da   ras - tat.
i   ji - vo - ta   vred da   ou - kras - sia - vat.

Gréï - na - li   lă - či   na - vred.   Bis - tro

iz - vor - čè   chour - ti.   Ra - dost   bli - ka   v'çè - li

svet.   Ptič - ka   vès - sè - lo   lè - ti.

Every day in the early morning
We awaken to greet the sun.
The sunrays, the air and the dew
Bring joy to our hearts,
So that inspiring thoughts flow in our minds
Growing beautiful feelings in our hearts.
The brilliant rays shine everywhere,
A limpid spring streams down,
Joy flows over the whole world,
The birds are merrily flying around.

BEAUTY
Music and lyrics as Flexibility.

20. CONQUERING

Allegro

Dè - niat pri - sti - ga sled noch - ta, i ra - dost i - dè sled skrăb - ta. Văr - vi - mè ni po svèt - li păt, prè - gra - di nè - ma da ni sprat. Taï bez - spir - no chté văr - vi - mè s've - ra i liou - bov v'găr - di - té; kăm po - bè - di chté lè - ti - mè, do - kat glè - dat ni o - či - té. Bo - dro vdi - ga - mè če - la, smé - lo trăg - va - mè na - pred! Do - ri v'né - vo - lia i bè - da za nas è hou - bav Bo - ji svet. Mil - va ni ti - hi - iat zé - fir. Pé - iat ni ptič - ki s'vès - sèl glas. Leï sè v'dou - cha - ta è - li - xir pri iz - grèv slăn - çe v'ra - nen čas.

The day follows on from the night,
Joy follows on from sorrow.
We walk upon a luminous path,
No obstacle will make us stop.
That is how we will always proceed
With faith and love in our hearts
We will fly towards victory
Until we achieve our goal.
Our heads uplifted,
We bravely march ahead.
The sacred world retains its beauty,
Even in the hour of disaster and distress.
The air gently strokes us,
The birds sing us merry songs,
Our souls are filled with elixir
At dawn with the rising sun.

21. JOY OF THE EARTH

Li - kou-va çè - la - ta zé - mia i sè

rad - va ot sàr - çè. I ti - ča tia po svo - ia

pǎt ka - to dè - vi - ça vǎs - liou - bé - na. Tia ja -

- dou - va slǎn - çè - to i kǎm nè - go sè strè - mi.

To ia mil - va ot da - lèč i çè - lou - va

ia s'lǎ - či. Tia sè rad - va i mou peï:

«O, slǎn - çè na ji - vo - ta moï,

lè - tia, lè - tia kǎm tè - bè nè - pres - ta -

- no, i pǎl - na s'ra - dost. Ré - ki

té - kat, iz - vo - ri bli - kat čis - ti, vǎr - ho - vè

bè - lo - snej - ni vǎv ro - zo - vi si - ia - nia,

o - bli-vach i - zo - bil - no s'mi-louv - ki   néj - ni.»

The whole earth rejoices with gladness,
Wending on its way
Like a beloved maiden.
She is longing for the sun,
And stretches out towards him.
He caresses her from afar,
Strokes her with is rays.
She sings to the sun with delight:

Oh sun of my life,
I fly endlessly towards you.
And full of joy the rivers flow,
The streams are gently murmuring.
You shower the snow-capped peaks
With a rosy glint
And gentle touch.

22. ACQUAINTANCE

How pleasantly the small bird is singing,
And the sun is bountifully shining.
At dawn we dance and sing
In the dewy meadows and fields.
Life is beautiful and abundant,
Because GOD showers his kindness
upon us.

After the dancing and songs
We start working our earth.
We sow selected seed
So as to reap the wheat.
Gentle dew and rain will water them.
And the sun will help them grow.

23. Beautiful Day

Every beautiful day, the gift of GOD,
I breath the air of life and joy.
My face is always smiling.
Because GOD loves me.
The sun strokes my face with love.
The beloved voice of Christ
Whispers in my heart:
"Be firm and brave in life
And help the world.
With songs of joy
Glorify the love of GOD,
Our beloved and sacred Father
Who is known to us all".

24. HOW HAPPY WE ARE

Allegretto

Kol-ko smè do - vol - ni čé v' svè-ta ji - vé - èm! Ka - to ptič-ki vol - ni

čoud-ni pes-ni pé - èm. Sou-trin mi-lo slăn - çè po - srè-chta-mé ra - no.

To ni bla-go - sla - via i ji-vot ni da - va. Văz-douḫ di-cham bla-go-dat.

Ra-dost-no o - ti - vam za do - ma. Çé - la - ta pri - ro - da s'mè - nè pèï,

slăn - çè -to mé ji - vo greï. Men pri-ro-da-ta o - bi - ča

i v'ji-vo-ta mi po - ma - ga; čè - do svo-è mè na - ri - ča

i mi kaz-va dou - ma bla - ga: « Ra - bo - ti, ou - či, vrè-mè nè gou-bi,

vrè-mè nè pi - leï, skăp ji-vot pa - zi. Toï è Bo - ji dar, mil i skă-po-çen;

ti do-brè var-di go vsè - ki čas.» A po - dir i - gri - té

chté o - ti - da da ra - bo - tia, vrè - mè da né gou - bia,

dor v'né-bé - to slan - cè greï. Haï na - pred ed - no, dvè, tri

s'bo - dri   stăp - ki   ti   ho - di.   O - chtè   mal - ko   ni - é   touk

chtè si po - i - gra - é - èm sè - ga.   Ho - di, ho - di, ho - di,

za vo - da - ta ho - di,   prèz rè - či - ça bis - tra, po pă - té - ka čis - ta.

Ô vo - di - çé   slad - ka, ji - va,   nos - sich ti ji - vo - ta nov.
Teb o - bi - čam,   teb ja - dou - vam,   té - bé tăr - sia vsé - ki čas.

Po   li - va - di   i   gra - di - ni   né - prè - sta - no   ti - čach ti.
Taï   prèz vsi - čki - té   go - di - ni   bé - gaï, ti - čaï i   lè - ti.

How happy we are to live in this world!
We sing lovely songs like carefree birds!
In the early morning we meet the dear sun.
It blesses us and gives us life.
We breathe the rich and abundant air,
I return home with joy in my heart.
The whole of Nature sings with me,
I feel the living light of the sun.
Nature cherishes me and helps me in my life,
She calls me her dear child
And whispers softly to me:

"Work, study and don't waste time,
Guard your precious life,
It is a priceless gift from GOD.
Guard it carefully at all times."

After the dancing I shall go to work,
Without wasting any time,
Working as long as the sun shines.
Let's walk along with cheerful steps,
One, two, three.
We will dance here in a while.
Go, go, go along a clean path
And fetch water from a clear river.

Sweet living water,
You bring us new life.
You ceaselessly flow
Through meadows and gardens.

I love you, I long for you,
I search you out all the time.
Run, flow and fly
Through all the years to come!

25. STEP BY STEP

Stăp - ka po stăp - ka è - to ni   văr - vim kăm no - vi -

- ia   ji - vot.   Čer - ta-èm svè - tli bǎd - ni - ni   za nas i çel čo -

-vèch - ki rod.   Vsič - ki prè - gra - di   prè - o - do - lia - va - mè,

nè sè stra - hou - va - mè   ot   bè - di.   Mi - sli kras - si - vi

vrè - dom pos-sia - va - mé,   liou - bov své - ta   da   po - bè - di.

Pă - tè - ka svè - tla   è   pred nas   i no - va čoud - na

svèt - li - na.   Ji - vot v'săr - ça - ta   ni   sè vli - va,

mă - drost i liou - bov.   Pă - tè - ka svè - tla

è   prèd nas   i no - va čoud - na svè - tli-na.

Ji - vot v'săr - ça - ta ni   sè vli - va, mă - drost i liou -

- bov.   Çvè - tia - ta   ou - ha - iat,   zrè - iat plo - do -

- vé   Vsič - ko ras - tè, ji vè - è,   rad - va sé çé-li   mir.

Văz - douḫ   di - cham   a - ro -   mat,

vrè - dom   čoud - na   kra - so - ta.

Iz - vo - ri   bli - kat   čis - ta vo - da,

Bis - tra ros - sa   vsè - ko lis - to   săs   bri - liant kras -   si.

Step by step we walk towards the new life.
We draw out a bright future for ourselves
And all mankind.
We overcome all obstacles,
We are not frightened by disasters.
We sow beautiful thoughts all around,
So that sacred love will overcome.
A bright path opens up ahead of us,)
In a new and beautiful light.   ) Repeat
Life, love and wisdom   )
Flow into our hearts.   )

The flowers give out their scent.
The fruits are ripening,
Everything grows and lives,
The whole world rejoices.
We breathe the scented air,
With wonderful beauty everywhere.
Springs of pure water are whispering,
The clear dew adorns every leaf
Like a beautiful diamond.

26. EARLY IN THE MORNING

Koï na ra - ni - na sta - va da i - greï
po zè - lè - na - ta trè - va i na bis - tra - ta ros - sa,
toï chtè bă - dè več - no mlad, zdrav i hou - bav i bo - gat;
chtè sè ou - či naï do - brè, nè - ma niv - ga da ou - mrè.

Whoever gets up early and dances
On the green grass in the clear dew
Will always be young and healthy,
Beautiful and rich.
He will learn best of all
And he will never die.

27. DICHANÉ — RESPIRATION

Inspiration A . . . . Expir. Inspiration A . . . . Expir.

Inspiration A . . . . Expir.

28. PROVIDENCE

Da prèbădé Bojiat mir i da izgréè Bojiata radost
i Bojièto vessèliè v'nachité sărça!

May the Peace of GOD abide,
And May Divine Joy
And Divine Exultation
Arise in our hearts!

SUNBEAMS

Allegro

1. Зо-ра се е свет-ла за-зо-ри-ла, ти жи-во-та новъ е про-я-ви-ла,. Слън-чевъ та-нецъ в'пла-ни-на-та за-и-гра-ва-ме и за друж-но ний за-пѣ-ва-ме слън-че-ви-тѣ пѣс-ни.

2 Тѣ сърд-ца-та ни раз-тва-рятъ за лж-чи-тѣ, слън-це-то ни про-го-ва-ря чрезъ и-гри-тѣ. Новъ жи-вотъ ни то да-ря-ва, но-ва свѣт-ли-на,_ но-ва свѣт-ли-на. Скър-би зем-ни раз-то-пя-ва свой-та то-пли-на.

3 Вѣр-на стж-ка ти взе-ми, свѣт-ла ми-съль при-е ми; тя жи-вотъ ще ти да-ри, ра-дость но-ва и кра-си-ви бжд-ни-ни ще из-гра-ди. Вѣр-на стж-ка ти взе-ми, свѣ-тла ми-съль

1. Bright dawn is breaking,
Bringing forth the new life.
In the mountains we begin
Our sunlit dance,
Singing in harmony.

2. The sun communicates with us
Through our dances
Which open our hearts to its rays.
It endows us with the new life
And the new light.
It melts away earthly sorrows
With its warmth.

3. Take a true step,
Accept the radiant thought;
It will give us the gift of life.
It will build new joy and a beautiful future. (repeat)

4. We continually advance
In a brave and orderly way;
We send a powerful appeal
For a new and pure life.
Love and brotherhood are already
Coming into the world.

5. When the new life arises
In our world,
Every living being will sing for the sun.
Everyone will live in knowledge, love and freedom.

6. The new path is at hand:
Come out of the circle of limitation!
The radiant heavenly hosts are calling on you
Set out bravely towards the future,
And take the path to freedom!

7. Mother Earth, I was born of you
A beautiful being
Who will grow to be clever,
Thoughtful and loving.
This is the life of paradise......

8. Paradise (Raiee)...Paradise (16 times)
This is paradise, paradise, paradise.

9. Tell me, tell me two sweet words
Your two words
Sweet two words (repeat).

10. This is paradise. (repeat four times)

1. Zora se e svetla zazorila, tya jivota nov e proya-
vila. Slancev tanets v planinata zaigravame
i zadrujno nii zapyavame slantche vite pecni.

2. Te surdtsata ni raztvaryat za lutchite, slanceto ni progovarya
tchrez igrite. Nov jivot ni to daryava, nova svetlina,
nova svetlina. Skurbi zemni raztopyava svoita topli-
na. 3. Byarna stupka ti vzemi, svetla misul
priemi, tya jivot shte ti dari, radost nova i krasivi
budnini shte izgradi. Vyarna stupka ti vzemi, svetla misul
priemi; tya jivot shte ti dari, radost nova i krasivi
budnini shte izgradi. 4. Vsce napred v stroen rad smelo nii
trugvame napred.
kum jivot tchist i nov moshten zov
prashta me navred. (pred) ide vetch v svyata
bratstvo i lioubov bov. 5. V nashata zemya
nov jivot koga izgree vsitchko jivo shte zapee
za slanceto. V znanie, lioubov i svoboda vseki shte jivei. 6. putya nov
e gotov; ot kruga tesen islezni (ni)
Gore te zovat svetli visini; kum vurha
kum vuzhod v drujen hod smelo dnes trug-ni
ti kum svoboda putya poemi.
7. Ti ci me mamo tchovek kra-
siv rodila, umen da stana, dobre da
mislya, dobre da lioubya. Tui jivota e na
raya .... 8. Rai (16 times).....................
....
....Tui e rai,
rai, rai. 9. Kaji mi, kaji mi, kaji mi sladki dumi
dve dve. Tvoite dumi dve, sladki dumi
dve. Tvoite dumi dve, sladki dumi dve.
10. Tui e rai (four times), rai.

PENTAGRAM

Here we come,
Luminous rays,
Bearing a royal and blessed gift:
Joy, peace and love,
Light and living beauty,
And freedom to all noetic beings.

We are the rays of the sun of love,
We have come to earth to conquer evil
So as to establish peace.
With blessing, light and gentle love,
We will establish a new life
Throughout the world.